"The Spiritual Blueprint readings I received from Ed Tarabilda gave me an understanding of my spiritual nature and path that has guided me ever since. *Doorways to Awakening* offers that same gift. This is wisdom that will help every reader experience the profound grace of self-acceptance and self-love."

—Jennifer Read Hawthorne, #1 *New York Times* bestselling author, *Chicken Soup for the Woman's Soul*

"I was fortunate to receive a Spiritual Blueprint reading from Edward Tarabilda just before he left to play tennis the fateful morning of his transition (making me the last person to ever receive a reading from him). And, boy, did he get me right! His knowledge, wisdom, and perspective have been invaluable to me. I'm thrilled to endorse this book, as *Doorways to Awakening* gives you a practical roadmap to the various time-tested paths of awakening. This is a brilliant user manual for life."

—Marci Shimoff, #1 *New York Times* bestselling author, *Happy for No Reason* and *Chicken Soup for the Woman's Soul*

"Finally! I'm so excited to see Ed's profound and life changing insights in *Doorways to Awakening* being shared. Ed's reading for me changed the way I viewed my very existence and created a feeling within me of deep and lasting joy. Knowing one's Spiritual Blueprint will help anyone live a more Passionate life, a life in alignment with their highest purpose."

—Janet Bray Attwood – *New York Times* bestselling author of *The Passion Test* and *Your Hidden Riches*

"From the foundations of the Holy East I've found amazing insights and truths in this wonderful manuscript gently guiding the reader towards a life of awakened mastery. It's fascinating to explore the concept of planetary energies and how they affect us in real life. *Doorways to Awakening* clearly identifies the planetary energies that make up all of us, and the doorways each of these offer to assist us on our spiritual journey. This is a must read for anyone looking to grow, evolve and expand their consciousness."

—Rev. Julie Renee Doering - Master Quantum Health Activator, Brain Rejuvenation Expert

"I have always been a Bhakta, following the path of the Heart. *Doorways to Awakening* gives such a clear and compelling depiction of that journey, as well as all of the other pathways, giving everyone the opportunity to discover which resonates with him/her most powerfully.

I sincerely feel that this book will be of great value to many people, furthering our shared desire as a planetary collective, for the Awakening of All Beings!"

—Ariel Spilsbury, author of the *13 Moon Oracle* and *The Alchemy of Ecstasy*

Doorways to Awakening
A Guide to Self Realization

By Edward Tarabilda
and Orion Hawthorne

Lotus Press
P O Box 325
Twin Lakes, WI 53181 USA
www.LotusPress.com

Doorways to Awakening
A Guide to Self Realization
By Edward Tarabilda and Orion Hawthorne

First Edition, January, 2017

www.doorwaystoawakening.com

ISBN: 978-0-9406-7642-8

Cover Design: Lucinda Rae Kinch
http://prosperitybranding.com/

Publisher:
Lotus Press
P O Box 325
Twin Lakes, WI 53181 USA
www.LotusPress.com

Table of Contents

About Edward F. Tarabilda and Orion Hawthorne

Acknowledgments

Introduction.. 1

Chapter 1 - What is Awakening?.. 3

Chapter 2 - The Macrocosm/Microcosm Mirrors............. 9

Chapter 3 - Introduction to the Planets: Aspects of
Humanity.. 13

Chapter 4 - Introduction to The Fields of Living............. 17

Chapter 5 - The Power of Attention.................................. 19

Chapter 6 - Three Steps on the Spiritual Ladder............. 21

Chapter 7 - The Planets and Spiritual Paths.................... 27

- Saturn and The Path of the Physical Body, Hatha Yoga.......... 33
- Venus and The Path of the Senses, Raj Yoga........................... 43
- Mars and The Path of the Spiritual Warrior, Laya Yoga/Shakti
  Kundalini.. 55
- The Moon and The Path of Devotion, Bhakti Yoga................. 69
- Mercury and The Path of Intellectual Discernment, Gyan
  Yoga.. 77
- Jupiter and The Path of Selfless Service, Karma Yoga............ 89
- The Sun and The Integral Path, Surya Yoga........................... 101
- Rahu and Ketu – The North and South Nodes of the Moon
  and The Path of the Iconoclast, Tantra................................. 109
- Desire... 121
- Conclusion: Determining Your Spiritual Nature................... 125

Chapter 8 - The Fields of Living... 127

- Dharma, The Field of Caste Nature... 129
- Primal Desire, The Field of Wealth.. 135
- Relating Style, The Field of Relationships............................. 141
- Career Nature, The Field of Career... 147
- Creative Play, The Field of Recreation.................................... 151
- Mental Health, The Field of the Vital Body........................... 157
- Physical Health, The Field of the Physical Body.................. 165

Chapter 9 - Some Conditions that May Contribute to Awakening.. 167

Conclusion.. 179

About the Authors

Doorways to Awakening was prepared by Orion Hawthorne in collaboration with Edward F. Tarabilda (deceased).

Edward died of a sudden heart attack in early January, 1999 while playing tennis on the indoor tennis courts at Maharishi University of Management in Fairfield, Iowa.

Edward left a substantial body of research and volumes of case studies with Bernadette Cardinale, his beloved partner, creative director and teacher of the Art of Multi-Dimensional Living. Bernadette continued to research, refine, and edit the teachings of the spiritual science of the Art of Multi-Dimensional Living on which this book is based. In fact, much of this book is Edward's insights presented in his own words, which is why he is listed as first author. However, some of Edward's passages have been expanded, and there are some sections of the book including most of Chapters 1–6 and 9, which although partially inspired by him, are not his words. Additionally, some of Edward's passages have been edited for clarity and are organized in a more easy-to-comprehend fashion.

Edward Tarabilda

Edward F. Tarabilda cognized The Art of Multi-Dimensional Living®, the name given to the body of spiritual and applied knowledge he founded.

Edward was raised in a traditional Catholic family. After attending a minor Catholic seminary, college and law school, he became a lawyer and professor of law and government in Springfield, Illinois. His life underwent a profound change when he learned Transcendental Meditation® in the early 1970s and gained a Master's Degree in Vedic Science from Maharishi European Research University. He then became an Assistant Professor of Law and Government and Vice President of Maharishi International University in Fairfield, Iowa.

Edward's beloved partner, Bernadette Cardinale, also holds a Master's Degree in Vedic Science from Maharishi European Research University and she has taught Transcendental Meditation since 1974. Edward first met Bernadette on the campus of Maharishi International University.

In 1980 Edward began a more independent search for spiritual illumination which included the study of aspects of Vedic knowledge, such as Ayurveda, Jyotish, and Yoga. In addition to Eastern philosophy, Edward explored modern Western approaches to spiritual growth such as Anthroposophy.

By the late 1980s, Edward had cognized an approach to spiritual life that presented unique features in comparison with approaches taught in the name of spirituality then and up to the present. He named this teaching The Art of Multi-Dimensional Living® and he founded The New U™ to promote it.

Edward currently has two published books:

Ayurveda Revolutionized, Integrating Ancient & Modern Ayurveda, Lotus Press, 1997

The Global Oracle, 1st World Publishing, 1997

Orion Hawthorne

Orion (a.k.a. Daniel Hawthorne) graduated from Maharishi International University (now known as Maharishi University of Management) in 1979 with a Bachelor's degree in Western Philosophy and in 1981 with a Master's degree in Higher Education Administration.

He became a teacher of Transcendental Meditation in 1977 in Avoriaz, France and a Governor of the Age of Enlightenment in South Fallsburg, New York in 1979.

His spiritual journey led him to a profound awakening in the Presence of Gangaji in 1995.

He has been a technical writer for over 30 years.

Orion has recently co-offered a course on the Alchemy of the Sacred Inner Marriage with Sarah Uma, an ordained Priestess of the 13 Moon Mystery School and a Temple Keeper for the Sanctuary of the Open Heart. Orion has journeyed through two full cycles of the 13 Moon Mystery School with Ariel Spilsbury, its founder, as the focalizer.

Orion is the author or co-author of three other books already published or in process:

- *Alchemy of the Sacred Inner Marriage: A Journey of Self-Love and Awakening* (co-authored with Sarah Uma)

- *Annihilated by Love* (soon to be published)

- *Shiva's Guide to Awakening* (in process)

Acknowledgments

I am forever grateful to Bernadette Cardinale for entrusting me with Edward's writings, for her mentorship in the Spiritual Science of the Art of Multi-dimensional Living, and for her careful editing of this book. Without her inspired guidance this book would not have been possible.

A big, heartfelt Thank You to Nimueh Rephael for her detailed proofreading and to Jennifer Read Hawthorne for her guidance and support.

I also want to express my deepest gratitude to Maharishi Mahesh Yogi whose Transcendental Meditation® technique has been an invaluable part of my own spiritual life, and I believe has important spiritual and life benefits for all people.

And, deepest gratitude to Gangaji, whose Presence stopped my mind in its tracks and revealed the unspeakable, unimaginable Love of our Being.

And finally, I want to acknowledge and thank Sarah Uma, whose inspiration and Presence inspired me to finally write this book.

Orion
San Ramon, California
September 30, 2016

Introduction

*Kabir said, "I once experienced reality for fifteen seconds
and the rest of my life was spent in devotion to that."
He wasn't saying, "I tried to get another experience"
or "I worked to get another experience."
He said, "...the rest of my life was spent in devotion to that."*
– Gangaji

*The only obstacle (to Self Realization) is
the belief that there is an obstacle.*
– Papaji

To be happy, to realize the truth of who you are, needs nothing.
– Gangaji

*There are more things in heaven and earth, Horatio,
Than are dreamt of in your philosophy.*
– Shakespeare, *Hamlet* (1.5.167-8), Hamlet to Horatio

The primary purpose of this book is to enliven the desire for awakening... to light the fire and fan the flames. The most important things you can get from this book are:

- an experience of the silent witness within and the understanding that this is your true, essential nature,
- an awareness of all of the spiritual paths to Self Realization and how you can continually advance or evolve,
- a fervent desire to awaken or deepen within one's awakening,
- a continual openness and honesty regarding what contributes most, and
- an exploration of practical methods that may assist and hasten your awakening, or an even deeper level of awakening.

Of course, everything contributes to some extent. However, the elements of each of the generalized paths described in this book have been shown over time to have value in speeding things up. You must decide for yourself which path and which elements of that path contribute most at any given moment or period in your life. For this, no formula can be offered, other than to follow one's own inner guidance. Let the law of attraction be your guide.

And yet, there is one specific spiritual path that will likely contribute more consistently and more effectively to your advancement than any other. A person's Spiritual Blueprint™ indicates which path is the primary one for that person.

For details on how to receive your individualized Spiritual Blueprint™ reading go to

doorwaystoawakening.com/spiritual-blueprints/

Chapter 1
What Is Awakening?

What is Awakening?

Awareness of awareness itself as one's true and eternal identity. One's body, mind, sense perceptions, roles, life circumstances are clearly perceived as ever changing phenomena.

And what is the value of awakening?

In a word, Freedom. Freedom from all of the changing circumstances and roles in life. Freedom from the constant chatter of the mind. Freedom from being at the effect of our body, our changing moods, or the dictates of our mind. When we know ourselves to be the Silent Witness within that is aware of the mind's chattering and our changing moods, then we are no longer at the effect of them. These thoughts and moods are observed, or witnessed, as changing phenomena within the field of consciousness.

And what arises is:

The experience of connection with All That Is.

Inner Peace.

Fulfillment beyond the circumstances of life.

When an individual is no longer identified with everchanging thoughts, emotions, or circumstances of life but recognizes they are in truth the silent, still awareness witnessing it all, the universal awareness from which individual mind emanates, this is called "awakening."

Awakening is not just having the thought, "I am universal awareness."

Awakening is awareness watching individual thoughts and realizing "I am not that thought." I am the silent, still awareness that is watching every thought. And these thoughts are just momentary energetic phenomena which arise within awareness. With this awareness of pure awareness beyond all thought, we cease identifying with our thoughts, our emotions, our mind. And the seed of awakening has been planted.

When awareness recognizes that it is not a limited individual, that it is no thing at all, like the vast blue sky, then each passing cloud of thought is recognized to be insubstantial and relatively inconsequential. Awareness is not identified with any thing or as anything at all. There is simply no identity. There is no identifying with the sky of awareness, nor with the witness of thoughts, nor with the thoughts, nor the emotions, nor the personality, ego, or body. There is simply no identification at all. Identification is also a thought.

"Awakening" is a word which points to a condition of nonidentification with anything whatsoever. What gets awakened? The individual consciousness as it cuts the cord of identification with its thoughts, moods, roles, circumstances, and its body.

In this grand illusion, the Leela of manifest creation, that which is Real, that which is unchanging, pure Awareness, appears and is revealed in the midst of everchanging thoughts, forms, and phenomena. This we call "Awakening."

Awakening is, somehow, miraculously and wonderfully, a byproduct of grace. Awakening is not a goal. Awareness is, and always has been, who we all are. That which is revealed, Awareness or Self, is all that is Real. It is this moment. Awakening is a moment-to-moment realization, and the surrender of all that appears, back to this moment, its source.

Awakening is also called Self Realization or Enlightenment. It is realizing the silent Self within as the common denominator of all experience, the silent witness. When the clouds of thoughts are removed, the Sun can then shine forth unobstructed. The Sun (Self) has always been there, though it is easily overlooked when obscured by clouds (thoughts). This is why having repeated experiences of pure awareness, which is awareness without thoughts, or awareness in which thoughts are greatly diminished or dissipated, is essential to awakening from identification with the constant mindstream of thoughts that have a tendency to obscure it. However, awareness is always there in the midst of all experience, and just requires turning our attention to it to realize it as one's essential nature.

Thoughts come and go, but awareness goes on, silently witnessing the whole phenomenal display.

What is it to be identified? When we identify with our body or mind, for instance, we experience that who we are is nothing other than the body, or the mind, or the roles we play in life. And with this identification, when these things change, as they inevitably will, we suffer.

Some people even identify with their cars or the beer they drink or the teams they route for. Ha! As though being a 'Cadillac driver', or a 'Budweiser drinker', or an 'Oakland Raiders fan' means something about them, their status in life.

And, many people identify with their roles... mother, father, computer programmer, teacher, student, and on and on.

But what lies beyond all of these roles, these labels we give ourselves? Who is that silent witness within that observes each thought as it arises, who is the same throughout all of the circumstances of life?

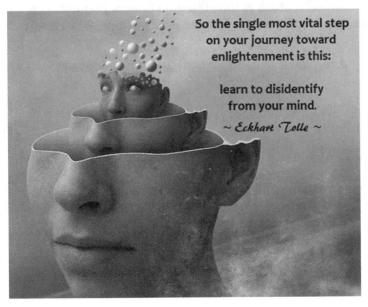

So the single most vital step on your journey toward enlightenment is this:

learn to disidentify from your mind.

~ Eckhart Tolle ~

Upon Awakening, that which one awakens to (who one is, Self, the stillness at the core of one's Being), emerges. It goes from being in the background, overshadowed by the constant activity of the mind, to being present along with all experience.

Life before awakening is like experiencing the numerator of a fraction only, the top highly variable number. Upon awakening, suddenly the denominator that has been hidden, now appears. And in this case, it is truly the common denominator. One!

Awakening is Awareness becoming aware of itself, Self-Aware.

Awareness, Self, is omnipresent, the baseline or common denominator upon which all experience appears. It is the blank slate, like a blank movie screen onto which our life stories, the people and circumstances of our lives, appear.

This is why, when we realize awareness as our essential nature, as the truth of who we are, the stable ground onto which all experience is projected, then we cease to be identified with all of the changing phenomena of experience. Our thoughts (which we call our mind), our emotions, our body, or any of our roles or circumstances, all of these changing phenomena come and go while awareness itself remains unchanged.

This is why awareness is also called the Self. It is our true Self. It is not our personality self, which is something that develops and changes over time. Rather, it is our true, unchanging Self, awareness itself.

This is why when a person becomes aware of awareness itself, he is said to be Self Realized. He has now realized the nonchanging aspect of his/her Self.

And, upon Self Realization a person experiences freedom. True freedom. Freedom from attachment to any of the changing phenomena of life. Free from identification with his/her personality, mind, emotions, body, circumstances.

Of course, personality, mind, emotions, body, circumstances still occur, but now to the backdrop of stillness, of silence, of awareness itself. And these changing phenomena are no longer taken quite as seriously. There is now an experience of some degree of detachment from this changing field of life that was formerly all that we knew.

So, now the question arises, how can anything done on the relative, changing level of existence, the field of cause and effect, reveal that which is beyond cause and effect?

Awareness is like the clear blue sky which has been obscured by the clouds, the clouds of experience, the clouds of thought. All that is required to allow awareness to shine through is to dissipate the clouds, even a little bit.

As every action has a reaction, every thought simply sets in motion another thought. And yet, somehow, the miracle of creation is that energy (including the energetic phenomenon of thought) dies out. It can dissipate. Thoughts do dissipate, and the mind can come to rest.

Wherever there is a mind, there is the possibility of no mind. Wherever there are thoughts, there is the possibilty of no thought, of even momentary annihilation of the mind. What is the mind? Thoughts occurring moment-to-moment, and in this moment lies the possibility of no thought whatsoever, and what this reveals: the silence, presence, peace at the core of one's being, all being, which is never not present, even along with, and as, every thought, even in the midst of the most intense mental activity. Awareness simply becomes apparent when thought dissipates.

""Who awakens? Consciousness wakes up to itself. That is who you are.

"It may not be who you think you are. We have objectified ourselves as this particular body, or the sensations that go through the body, or our emotions, or our history. But those are all objects in our minds. They are thoughts, concepts.

"True awakening is the recognition that those objects are made of nothing, no substance. And yet they are never separate from the subjective, endless consciousness that one is.

"So, who awakens? You awaken! And you are already awake as consciousness. That is the paradox.

"However it is spoken of, the truth cannot be caught in a concept. But it can be realized, and that is who you are." -Gangaji

Self Realization is not Self Esteem

Self Realization is not the same as self esteem which has become very popular these days, as the benefits of having self-esteem are indisputable. A strong self-esteem is a by-product of a strong Sun (our inner essence) though, so they are related. We will delve into this connection later in this book.

Self Love, a heightened sense of self-esteem, is a strong sense of our individuality and appreciation of our uniqueness. It is self confidence, and it feels really good. Self Love is universal. Loving my self (my personality, my individual expression, me) is fun. However, there is something more, something that lies beyond and infuses and informs the personal expression of me (you), which is the universal aspect of Me (you, us All) that is even more fulfilling. And that something is what we call our true Self, awareness itself.

It is through transcending our individual ego that the universal light of the Sun (pure awareness, Presence, call it what you will) shines forth.

Chapter 2
The Macrocosm/Microcosm Mirrors

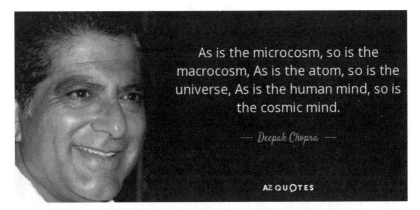

As is the microcosm, so is the macrocosm, As is the atom, so is the universe, As is the human mind, so is the cosmic mind.

— Deepak Chopra —

AZ QUOTES

Everything is energy. What does that mean? On the subtlest level of manifest creation, everything is made up of atomic and sub-atomic particles, which have both a wave and a particle nature. In essence, they are vibrating fields of energy.

All things are vibrating energy fields in ceaseless motion. The chair you sit on, the book you are holding in your hands appear solid and motionless only because that is how your senses perceive their vibrational frequency; that is to say, the incessant movement of the molecules, atoms, electrons, and subatomic particles that together create what you perceive as a chair, a book, a tree, or a body. What we perceive as physical matter is energy vibrating (moving) at a particular range of frequencies. Thoughts consist of the same energy vibrating at a higher frequency than matter, which is why they cannot be seen or touched. Thoughts have their own range of frequencies, with negative thoughts at the lower end of the scale and positive thoughts at the higher. Eckhart Tolle, *A New Earth*, pages *146-147.*

The macrocosm/microcosm dichotomy is an ancient Greek Neo-Platonic schema of seeing the same patterns reproduced in all levels of the cosmos, from the largest scale (macrocosm or universe-level) all the way down to the smallest scale (microcosm or sub-sub-atomic or even metaphysical level). In that system the midpoint is Man, who summarizes the cosmos.

The Greeks were philosophically concerned with a rational explanation of everything and saw the repetition of the Golden Ratio throughout the

9

world and all levels of reality as a step towards this unifying theory. In short, it is the recognition that the same traits appear in entities of many different sizes, from one man to the entire human population.

A **fractal** is a mathematical set that typically displays self-similar patterns. Fractals may be exactly the same at every scale, or they may be nearly the same at different scales. The concept of fractals extends beyond self-similarity and includes the idea of a detailed pattern repeating itself.

So, we begin our examination of our inner realm with an examination of what the outer, visible world has to offer us. If ultimately everything that is, is a phenomenon within the field of consciousness, an impulse of consciousness, then the experience we have of having an inner realm, the one in which thoughts occur, and an outer realm, the realm our sense perceptions reveal to us, can be seen as a continuum, rather than as two distinct fields. In other words, everything is a vibration of consciousness. Everything in the apparent outer world can be seen as an archetype or representation of what is occurring in our inner world, whether conscious or unconscious.

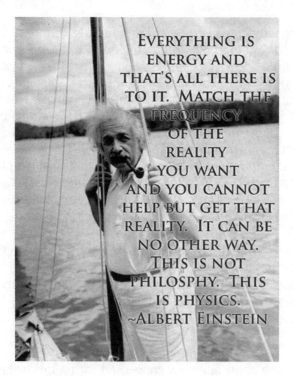

In this book we will explore the powerful aspects of our selves, the energies we call 'the planets'. The planets are not just physical entities in space. They are also powerful qualities of consciousness, qualities of awareness, which we experience as very specific aspects of our Being. These powerful energies are there in support of our soul's awakening. Our Spiritual Blueprint™, as well as our Vedic Astrology chart, gives us useful tools to assist in awakening.

And, miraculously, the position of the planets at the moment of our birth reflects the inner configuration and strength of all of these qualities within us. At the moment of our birth, all of the planets were in exact locations in the sky, creating an energetic matrix, an energy field, that is a macrocosmic representation of the microcosmic reality and is reflected in the human beings who are born at that moment.

Looking from the inside out, a person is born at the moment that the planets are in a configuration that is ripe for his/her birth that is resonant with him/her at a fundamental level. At this moment of resonance, our soul, our inner essence, manifests and we are born into this world. Because of this, the configuration of the planets in the sky at the moment of our birth provides us with a Spiritual Blueprint™ of our own energy configuration. Discovering our Spiritual Blueprint™ is a key to greater Self knowledge and offers an opportunity, a doorway into the transcendence of our own limited experience of everyday life, a doorway to our awakening.

Edward Tarabilda discovered this Spiritual Blueprint™. He realized there are eight archetypal spiritual paths which correspond to the planets, a historic discovery of incalculable value. He showed how all fields of living fit together into a seamless whole, united by the archetypal energies of the planets which underlie our subjective and objective universe. And, his theory blends smoothly into practice. The knowledge of the Spiritual Blueprint™ has had inestimable value for many people.

This book explores these basic planetary archetypal energies in their fundamental nature. We recommend a meditative or contemplative approach to reading it. If you rush through trying to stuff your brain with maximum information in minimum time, you will gain nothing except mental clutter. Memorizing facts without relating them to your own experience or daily life will be of little value to you. It is totally contrary to holistic development, which requires more attention to your inner experience than to any information gained from outside.

11

Please contemplate these planetary archetypes as vibrant, living realities, completely invisible yet manifesting everywhere. This book reveals the spiritual blueprint of the cosmos and its relationship to daily living, including the powerful planetary doorways to awakening.

Chapter 3
Introduction to the Planets:
Aspects of Humanity

As human beings, we all have the same fundamental aspects to our makeup. We all have bodies, a subtle body (chakras, our will power), senses, mind, intellect, heart, desire, and most of us have some sense of something greater than us, some intuitive wonder at the vastness of all of this creation of which we are a part, and some sense of awe and wonder. We call this 'connection with spirit', our religious nature, and our sense of justice and morality.

As we begin to awaken, all of these aspects of our Being are enlivened and called into play. Our Spiritual Blueprint™ brings awareness to these various aspects and provides a roadmap to their enlivenment. To bring wholeness to all that we are as human beings, we want to be aware of all of these aspects, to bring them all into their highest potential, and to transcend them to realize that which is beyond all of these traits. In this way, knowledge of one's Spiritual Blueprint™ provides a valuable paradigm and tool for Awakening.

One of the primary values of knowing your Spiritual Blueprint™ is Self knowledge; to become aware of all aspects of your Being, and to transcend them into the vastness of awareness, the silent Presence that knows itself as knowingness itself. It is the 'planets' as archetypal representations of each of these aspects that inform our own inner evolution and provide the keys to transcendence.

How can we use our knowledge and experience of these energetic aspects of ourselves we call 'planets' to assist us in awakening ever more fully? First, let's take a look at these aspects.

These 'planets' are:

Saturn: our body, our physical reality, and also our sleep-like nature, that which procrastinates and perceives obstacles. It is also that part of us that wants to go inward, to be alone, in solitude. Stillness, stability, longevity, constancy, durability, realism.

Venus: our senses, sight, sound, touch, taste, smell... and also our aesthetic sense, our sense of beauty, our romantic nature, romantic love, sexuality, and all aspects of the senses, sensuality.

Mars: our will power, our strength of will, determination, our warrior nature, that allows us to overcome all obstacles and to persevere. Also our prana, our breath, our subtle bodies (chakras), our dynamism and life force.

The Moon: our Heart which we experience as emotions. In its purest sense we experience The Moon as *agape* (Greek, universal love) Love, universal Love for all things, Mother Love, nurturing energy, our right brain intuitive and artistic nature, the creative aspect of our Being.

Mercury: our left-brain, analytical nature, which allows us to reason, and also to formulate language. Mercury also is experienced as our intellect, that which distinguishes this from that. It is organizing power, creative intelligence, detail orientation.

Jupiter: our spiritual nature, our sense of justice, our sense of fairness, of goodness, of what is right, our big picture awareness that allows us to see things in a holistic way and as interconnected, wisdom, our connection with Source, our religious sense.

The Sun: that which we experience as our self-confidence, our self-esteem, our inner essence, pure awareness.

Rahu: desire, our rebelliousness nature, that part of us that wants to shun authority and to rebel against the status quo, to break the boundaries of stagnation and conditioned existence and break out of the routine of life.

Ketu: represents karma and spirituality. Ketu signifies the spiritual process of the refinement of materialization to spirit. It is considered a benefic spiritually and a malefic materially as it causes sorrow and loss which often turns a person away from the outer, material world and inward to the silent witness, the silent Presence within. Ketu is considered responsible for Self Realization. Ketu is an indicator of intelligence, wisdom, non-attachment, mystic scientist, esoteric occultism, spiritual pursuits, liberation, penetrating insight, and psychic abilities.

Next, let's take a look at the different Fields of Living which these planetary energies influence.

Chapter 4
Introduction to the Fields of Living

Each planet occupies and therefore primarily influences one of our Fields of Living. What are the Fields of Living?

- Spiritual Nature: the way each of our minds transcend to realize our essential nature as awareness most easily and fully.
- Dharma: also known as our Caste nature.
- Primal Desire Nature: also called the field of 'wealth', one's primary desire in life.
- Relating Style: the way we relate to other people, our interpersonal interactions.
- Career Nature: the type of career or role we are best suited for.
- Creative Play: how we re-create and renew ourselves, and our relationship with children.
- Mental Nature: our personality and vitality.
- Physical Nature: our physical body type and health.

Which planet occupies each of these fields indicates fundamental differences of approach in that area of life. We will delve more deeply into each of these fields in Chapter 8.

Chapter 5
The Power of Attention

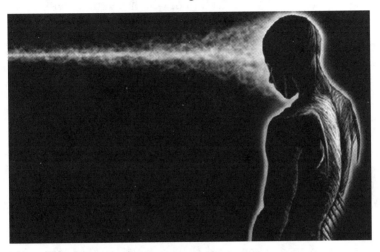

What we put our attention on grows stronger in our lives.

Perhaps you have heard this ancient adage?

The most powerful aspect of our Being is our attention. When we give something our attention, it grows. You have heard the expression, 'He sure does make a mountain out of a molehill.' That describes the experience of taking that one crumb on the kitchen counter and making it into the absolute most important thing that has ever happened in the universe.

It is our attention directed towards each of the planets and delving into the energy that each is, that activates them in our awareness and brings forth their potential energy to assist in awakening, or in furthering our evolution.

One of the values of identifying these energies, is gaining mastery.... And what is 'mastery' in this context? It is not what is normally meant by 'mastery', which is control over. The mastery we are speaking of is to learn how to identify and flow with these energies, to dance with them, to use them in support of our lives and our awakening. For instance, when we are experiencing one obstacle (Saturn) after another, after another to the fulfillment of our desires (Rahu), we have a choice. We can either summon up our will power to overcome these obstacles (Mars), or we can surrender the desire itself (Ketu).

Karate provides us with a good analogy. Masters of Karate, rather than using force to subdue their foes, learn to flow with the energy and to navigate within it. Sometimes what is called for in life is summoning up one's will power (Mars) to overcome the lethargy (Saturn) in the name of justice (Jupiter). Other times, what is called for may be to allow and appreciate the beauty and perfection of what is (Venus), with no need to change it.

As we become aware of these fundamental planetary energies within us, and enliven them through the power of our attention, we can use them to awaken and to flow more skillfully with all of life.

And, it is by bringing our attention to awareness itself that we enliven and stabilize it in our experience.

Awareness is. It is essence radiating forth from within each and every one of us. It is who we are, manifesting in a multitude of forms. What obscures the realization of ineffable awareness as who we are? It is so easily overlooked. Virtually all of our attention in life is outer directed, towards experience and the objects of experience, the senses, our thoughts, our emotions. Bringing our attention to awareness itself is all that is required to awaken. And these planetary doorways which are aspects of all of our makeup as human beings can bring us into a deeper and more fulfilling experience of our essence as awareness.

What brings about this awakening to our own inner essence? And what further obscures it? This is the journey we are all on. Once you have had a glimpse of this inner radiance, what allows that radiance to become primary in your experience? What brings that inner silence to the foreground of experience? These are the questions we must all ask ourselves to more fully awaken, and to be ruthlessly honest with ourselves about this.

Chapter 6
Three Steps on the Spiritual Ladder

Edward noticed that there appear to be three distinct stages of spiritual development, three steps on the spiritual ladder. He identified these stages as:

Stage 1 - The Stage of Religion: the refinement and development of character through moral and ethical prescriptions and commandments. The belief that God is separate from man, the creator is separate from his creation.

Stage 2 - The Stage of Yoga and Mysticism: meditative practices to further strengthen, purify, and integrate the mind and body. This is the stage of the spiritual seeker in which a person seeks to know God experientially.

Stage 3 - The Stage of Wisdom: realization of our true nature as described by the great spiritual teachers and traditions. An experience of the silent, still Presence within as the Source.

This book is primarily for those on Stage 2 of the spiritual ladder, the stage of the spiritual seeker. For people at this stage, this book will serve as a spiritual roadmap.

For those who are on Stage 3 of the spiritual ladder, the Stage of Wisdom, these 'paths' are known as one's spiritual expression. There is no longer a path, as at this stage one has arrived. However, these flavors of spiritual awareness are still experienced, and enjoyed, as delightful spiritual expressions, and the opportunity for deepening is never-ending.

Edward identified eight distinct types of mind, eight ways in which the mind can transcend itself. Although an individual mind may find it transcends from time to time in all of the ways, Edward hypothesized that each mind has one way that is its primary, or most effective way that it dissolves.

These eight "paths", or ways in which a mind dissolves while we are still awake, are:

Path of the	Vedic Name	also known as	Planet
Body	Hatha Yoga	The Path of Physical Purification	Saturn
Mind	Karma Yoga	The Path of Selfless Service	Jupiter
Senses	Raja Yoga	The Path of the Senses	Venus
Heart	Bhakti Yoga	The Path of Devotion	Moon
Will, chakras	Laya Yoga	The Path of the Spiritual Warrior	Mars
Intellect	Gyan Yoga	The Path of Intellectual Discernment	Mercury
All of the above	Surya Yoga	The Integral Path	Sun
Desire	Tantra	The Path of the Iconoclast	Rahu/Ketu

We will discuss each of these paths in detail. Then we will examine the remaining seven Fields of Living to give a complete picture of all aspects of life and their primary influences.

Although all three steps to some extent cultivate the will, the feelings and the mind, the first step is predominantly oriented to the will, the second to feelings, and the third to the mind.

Each of the three stages have individual variations.

The Stage of Religion

The first stage of spiritual development, the Stage of Religion, is the field of character development. It will be carried out predominantly through one of five different angles or approaches (see the Field of Living known as Caste/Dharma). The true purpose of religion is first, to bring character development and second, to lead one to the second stage, the stage of the spiritual seeker. Good fortune comes to he who learns to control the pleasures of the senses (Venus). This is the purpose of the first rung of the ladder, the path of religion, the path of moral and ethical development.

The Stage of Yoga and Mysticism

The stage of Yoga and Mysticism includes eight possibilities.

At this stage an individual ego begins to see the importance of sacrificing itself for the well-being of others and for spiritual advancement. The fundamental duality of self and others begins to be bridged. One increasingly begins to share one's life with others.

The growth which comes from this process is primarily on the level of feeling rather than will, and takes place through inward contemplation and meditation. Some call this second step on the spiritual ladder the path of Yogic practice; others call it the stage of mysticism, with its emphasis on mystical experiences (feeling level). The desire to share artistic impulses arises at this level of development.

This stage begins the process of ego dissolution. What is the key for accomplishing this? It is through Yoga, the second step of the ladder in spiritual development. *Yoga* means to yoke, to bind together, to unite. The beginning of all yoga is Karma Yoga, the path of selfless service and giving to others.

The Stage of Wisdom

The stage of Wisdom is more universal. Our experience of it will be colored by our spiritual nature and its related yogic disposition. The individual ego dissolves into the experience of the oneness of the Self. Its approach to the spiritual life is rigorously scientific, although it soon outstrips the rational, logical thinking of objective science. It moves from logic to intuition to insight as it passes through the religious, the mystical, and the philosophic phases of thinking. What starts as science eventually becomes religion, and when this true religious person looks back on the earlier religious phase, it is now seen as scientific. Thus, the strange workings of science, art, and religion in the life of the seeker and spiritual adept.

Every seeker of Truth begins with the stage of religion and the development of character. On this first step of the spiritual ladder the development of will is the primary focus.

The seeker then graduates to the stage of mysticism with its trance states and ecstatic feelings. On this second step of the spiritual ladder the heart and feelings are the primary focus.

The third and crowning step is the stage of wisdom. Insight is its outcome.

The path of religion, the path of meditative mysticism, and the path of higher knowledge are the three universal steps on the ladder of evolution.

Yoga, with its eight limbs, encompasses the first and second steps of the spiritual ladder, but not the third – except in the most rudimentary form. The practice of Yoga requires a sense of doership, agency, and control. These are the very qualities abrogated on the third step of the spiritual ladder.

The more selfish pleasures of the first stage are transformed into the more altruistic pleasures in the second stage. However, this process only reaches completion when wisdom dawns on the third rung of the ladder and egoism is completely transcended.

On the second step of the spiritual ladder, the individual experiences a strange mix of altruistic and selfish motives. Self-delusion often takes place through various forms of spiritual materialism.

The second step of the spiritual ladder is mystical in orientation; it is based in emotion and feeling.

The path of religion associated with the first step on the ladder of spiritual development is the religion of moral codes, dogma, and institutional forms. The religion associated with the second step is that of self-generated, inspired 'faith, hope and charity'.

The religion of the first step disciplines the will; the religion of the second step cultivates feeling; the religion of the third step is wisdom combined with the feeling of devotion.

At level one of the spiritual ladder, religion seeks to give the seeker a place of temporary rest and relaxation from the fast-paced life in the material world. It also seeks to provide a code of ethics to harness the will. This form of religion emphasizes external form and periodic retreat from the world.

On the first rung of the ladder, prayer is filled with effort; on the second rung it becomes an act of surrender.

Whether one consciously focuses on spiritual development or not, these three steps apply. If we make no effort for spiritual development, Nature guides our evolution in a slow, sequential, unconscious, and often circuitous path through the three phases. We must master moral development (Stage 1) before meditative practice becomes effective (Stage 2), and we must be adept meditators before direct wisdom dawns (Stage 3). However, we can accelerate the unconscious process through

24

conscious attention to spiritual development, simultaneously exercising heart, mind, and will on all three stages together.

The second stage of the spiritual ladder helps us climb to higher and higher levels of mystical feeling. However, these mystical feelings are not stable or permanent. Love keeps seeking a higher ground. There we find the Real, the wisdom that is always with us.

Chapter 7
The Planets and Spiritual Paths
Meet Your Favorite Deities

"The subjective spiritual blueprint should be treated as a scientific hypothesis rather than as established fact, and it is certainly offered in that spirit." – Edward Tarabilda

And, how do you test this hypothesis? With your own personal experience.

We invite you to be completely honest with yourself. Do any of these spiritual paths and the techniques or practices they espouse silence or dissipate the seemingly constant chatter of the mind?

Do they create within you the awareness of awareness itself, of that silent witness that can stand back and observe each thought? Do they, either immediately or over time, stabilize the experience of this witness, thereby cutting the cord of identification with the mind?

This is a personal matter. Only you can know what is true for you in this regard.

And, to find out what works for you, here are some suggestions.

The Planets are archetypal representations of all the various aspects that make us up as human beings. They are the first and most essential energies in relative existence. They are the energies and archetypes of consciousness manifested as and in all aspects of us; body, mind, intellect, will, heart, and our spiritual nature, giving nature and rebellious nature. They are powerful, subtle energy fields that govern the way we experience life. They are filters of our experience. There is nothing in the universe not affected by a planetary influence.

Some ancient cultures believed that the planets are external manifestations of spiritual beings. When they referred to a particular planet, they were actually referring to the class of spiritual beings which lay hidden behind or within the external form of the planet.

Whether this anthropomorphic description of these 'energies' as 'living beings' appeals to you, or not, will depend on your spiritual nature. Just as Native Americans referred to the wind, and the sun and all of nature as living beings, these elemental forces can also, validly, be seen and experienced simply as impersonal, elemental forces of nature.

Bringing your attention to these aspects of your self enlivens and strengthens them. We all have all of these planetary energies as parts of us. They just show up differently for different people, varying in their strength and in what aspect of the personality they primarily influence. When you know the configuration of these energies in general in your life (as reflected by your Vedic Astrology natal chart and your Spiritual Blueprint™), and which of these planetary influences are strongest at any given time of your life (which is given by both your progression chart and in the transits at any moment in time), you will be better able to witness, appreciate and enjoy life to its fullest.

Just as we can learn a great deal about each path from studying each of the planets, the reverse is also true: We discover a great deal about each planet from studying the spiritual doorway (yoga) related to it. So, we will delve into the unique energies of each planet and the spiritual doorway it represents in this chapter. We will introduce you more fully to these aspects of yourself, which you already experience and know quite well. They are energies that make up all of us. These energies predominate in different parts of us all which we call the Fields of Living. And they shift in their predominance and strength at different times in our life.

As you read the descriptions of each of the planets and their spiritual paths, see if you can grok the unique energy of each. Edward provided a series of short descriptions of each of these energies of the planets, given here, to help you get a feel for these energies. These 'aphorisms' taken as a whole should give you a pretty good sense of each of these planetary energies.

We all have all of these energies within us to varying degrees, though some of them will be much more pronounced and some may be so weak as to be virtually indistinguishable. See if you can feel these energies within you, and see the value in enlivening them in your experience, though never to the exclusion of the other planetary energies. A whole, complete and happy individual will result from appreciating all of these energies and in doing so, allowing all of them to come into balance in our lives.

The Spiritual Paths

"What is my spiritual path?" This may be the most important question we can ask. With traditional social order unraveling at the seams and the environment in ever-deeper distress, the highest good we can realize is our own awakening. The realization of our own essential nature as consciousness is the link between humanity and divinity, the finite and the infinite. And the spiritual and New Age arenas are noisy and crowded. Many seekers remain confused by all of the options.

The concept of different paths for different psychophysical-spiritual types is common to all the great religious and spiritual traditions throughout the world. Although all eight aspects are found in everyone, each individual has one that is most predominant as an avenue for spiritual development.

These paths are presented here as fundamental archetypes. The seven planets plus the nodes are the basic organizing energies behind both subjective and objective creation.

The eight paths correspond to the eight aspects of human life:

1. The physical body, ruled by Saturn

2. The senses, ruled by Venus

3. The mind manas, ruled by Jupiter

4. The intellect buddhi, ruled by Mercury

5. The will, ruled by Mars

6. The heart, ruled by the Moon

7. The integrating factor or sense of "I-ness," ruled by the Sun

8. Our independent, rebellious nature, ruled by the Nodes of the Moon.

There are eight general paths to Self Realization and there is a planet associated with each of these paths. When we understand these eight

29

paths and the attributes of each, then we will at the same time grasp the essential nature and attributes of the planet associated with that path. The reverse also holds true: understand the attributes of a planet and you will understand the spiritual path related to it.

These eight paths are most often referred to by their Vedic names, because the knowledge of each path is best preserved within this tradition. However, these paths are universal and are part of every spiritual tradition, even if we must dig deep within many of these traditions to find the various paths.

These paths are:

Path	Vedic Name	Planet	Area of Life
The Path of Physical Purification	Hatha Yoga	Saturn	Body
The Path of the Senses	Raja Yoga	Venus	Senses
The Path of the Spiritual Warrior	Laya Yoga	Mars	Will, chakras
The Path of Devotion	Bhakti Yoga	Moon	Heart
The Path of Intellectual Discernment	Gyan Yoga	Mercury	Intellect
The Path of Selfless Service	Karma Yoga	Jupiter	Mind
The Integral Path	Surya Yoga	Sun	All of the above
The Path of the Iconoclast	Tantra	Rahu/Ketu	Desire

The eight major planets of ancient lore point to the spiritual beings which lie within these bodies.

What planet predominates in our Spiritual Nature determines the way we will most effectively transcend the mind and realize pure awareness as our essential nature. However, all of the planetary energies are alive within all of us, each predominantly influencing a different area of our lives. Which planet predominates in our Spiritual Nature and which predominate in each area of our life are given by our Spiritual Blueprint™.

Determining our Spiritual Blueprint is not an exact science. At the time of Edward's transition, he felt he had found the exact determination of an individual's spiritual nature, as well as what planet primarily governs each area of an individual's life, the Fields of Living. However, he always regarded this determination as hypothetical, as informed guidance to be tested with our personal experience.

Since Edward's ascension, Bernadette Cardinale, Edward's beloved partner and Spiritual Science and Consciousness researcher, has received additional insight regarding the proper method of determining one's spiritual nature, and one's entire Spiritual Blueprint™ which includes all of the Fields of Living, which many people feel is even more accurate.

You may receive an individual Spiritual Blueprint™ reading from either Bernadette or Orion. In this reading you will be given your unique Spiritual Nature, as well as where each of the planets resides in each of your Fields of Living, revealing to you the primary influence, or perspective, you have in that field.

doorwaystoawakening.com/spiritual-blueprints

However, in addition to your being given this individualized reading, we encourage you to read the different spiritual paths and see for yourself which one (or ones) resonate most for you. Be ruthlessly honest with yourself. Which of these approaches gives you the best results?

SATURN

Saturn governs physical matter, deep sleep and the body. It is slow, dense and grounded energetically. It can also create obstacles to progress, to accomplishment, allowing us to slow down, develop patience, and turn our attention inward. It is also our lethargic nature, that which procrastinates and perceives obstacles and that part of us that wants to go inward, to be alone, in solitude. Stillness, stability, longevity, constancy, durability, realism.

Attributes

Saturn is patient, persevering, calm, and conservative in nature. Saturn is the most concrete and physical planetary energy. It likes clear, well-defined structure and boundaries.

Relative life is bound in time, space, and causation.

As Lord of Time, Saturn sets boundaries in time by delaying fulfillment of desires. Such delays occur only when we fail to live fully in the present; they help us learn to live in the present, the only time frame in which real joy can be experienced.

As ruler of the body, Saturn sets boundaries in space by defining our physical structure.

Finally, as Lord of Karma, Saturn sets boundaries in causation by determining the exact reaction for every action. In brief, Saturn helps us step off the stimulus-response treadmill and bring spirituality into the physical.

Saturn beings are people who have Saturn as an especially strong energy in their makeup. They tend to be very private by nature. Saturn likes to retire from the world and its incessant activity.

Do you want to go back to the land, find your roots, and feel the earth? Do you yearn for quiet time in nature, away from the hustle and bustle of city life? Do you believe less is more, and shun the commotion and complexity of modern living? Do you prefer precise, logical talk to vague, dreamy speculation?

If so, then Saturn is speaking through you. Saturn is so practical and down-to-earth that it doesn't drift off in the wild flights of fantasy characteristic of some of the more imaginative archetypes, such as Venus. But it has an enormous influence in our materialistic science-infatuated culture.

In the planetary family, Saturn is the Servant. Being a servant does not necessarily mean being servile, although the heavy sense of duty, responsibility, and guilt often carried by Saturn can lead to this result. Ideally, Saturn is the person who loves to serve others, who loves to take on difficult or onerous tasks which everyone else finds too difficult, too boring and tedious, or beneath their dignity.

Saturnine beings are by nature very serious. They think in a logical and even mechanical way. Saturn has the ability to turn bits of information into a well-organized inspirational package. The thinking of someone under the influence of Saturn tends to be somewhat mechanical. He or she builds knowledge piece by piece, in a very logical and orderly way. Saturnine beings are hungry for information. They are capable of creating an inspirational whole by bringing order to bits of information. Computers reflect this style of thinking.

The indolence of Saturn can serve individuals well in the spiritual life; it tends to make them hermits or recluses. In the ancient days this reclusive path was most often associated with Hatha Yoga, the physical approach to spirituality.

When it is said that Saturn is lame, it means that Saturnine beings tend to undergo great hardship in their lives. They may suffer internally or through external crises and adversity. Saturn beings grow enormously through grief and suffering; they know how to transform it.

Saturn only seeks to control others in ways which protect its own psychological or physical boundaries. Their need for psychological protection can give them a fundamentalist tendency; their need for physical protection can make them cautious and conservative in behavior.

Saturn's nature is paradoxical: it seeks clear, definite boundaries, but since boundaries make us feel confined or trapped, Saturn also seeks to escape the very boundaries it has created

The abode of Saturn is sometimes referred to as a "filthy ground." This sounds like an awful condemnation, but in actuality it merely indicates that a person under the influence of Saturn is very earthy and can enjoy primitive conditions which others would find intolerable.

Mining or other forms of exploration under the earth fall under the dominion of Saturn.

This planet governs decayed, dried-up trees and vegetation. High, windy deserts are the haunts of Saturn.

Saturn governs anything old. It is the eldest of all the planets. For this reason Saturn also governs longevity.

When Saturn has temporal rulership for any duration, its effects are often delayed until the last part of the time period.

The likelihood of a successful marriage increases as a Saturn being gets older, but they will need a partner who gives them a lot of privacy and time alone. If you aren't comfortable with periods of long silence, then don't marry someone who has a predominantly Saturnine personality.

Saturn is the taskmaster only when we refuse to stay in the tranquil peace of the present moment.

Don't try to outlast a committed Saturnine being at the bargaining table!

Many of the artistic works labeled as "primitive" or "realistic" exemplify the spirit of Saturn and how it expresses itself.

The field of physical health and longevity is under the rulership of Saturn.

Art which emphasizes a stark realism is Saturnine at its root.

Terse writing is Saturnine.

Symbol

♄ Represents matter (cross) taking precedence over mind or human spirit (crescent).

Gemstone

Blue sapphire is the gemstone which propitiates Saturn.

Sound

By toning "u", as in "tomb," you gain a feeling for the energetics of Saturn.

Deity

Saturn's deity is Brahma.

Light

The higher vibrations of Saturn are grounded, detail-oriented, disciplined, stable and purposeful with a strong inner directedness.

Shadow

The shadow of Saturn is sloth and rigidity. The lower vibrations of Saturn are lethargic, procrastinate, stuck in their ways, fundamentalist, inflexible, narcissistic.

Examples

Abe Lincoln had a classic Saturnine physique – kind, warm, and lean.

The Path of the Physical Body
Hatha Yoga

The Path of the Physical Body uses the physical body as the primary tool for transcendence. It is the path of Saturn and is also known as Hatha Yoga.

Hatha Yoga is a path that most people are familiar with. It involves yoga postures in its purest form, but also could involve dance, or running or any form of transcendence of the mind through the body.

Hatha Yoga is far more than physical postures and purificatory regimes. It requires great restraint in all areas; physical, mental, and emotional.

The Hatha yogi seeks simplicity and solitude. Fasting of the five senses is an important part of Hatha Yoga. This can include periodic sexual fasting (abstinence), food fasting, fasting from speaking, sleep fasting on a full moon night or a Saturday night (Saturn rules Saturday), and even periodic visual fasting. This is the most austere path for the serious seeker. and the most universal one for the casual seeker because anyone can benefit from some physical purification, if not taken to extremes.

Breathing techniques (pranayamas) are an important part of Hatha yoga, and play a preparatory role in other paths, especially kundalini yoga. Breath is the delicate bridge between mind and body, the subtle link between subjectivity and objectivity. Breathing techniques offer great potential for purifying both mind and body, but malpractice can cause untold damage.

Advanced pranayamas cannot be learned from books. They require a skilled master. Unfortunately, there are few, if any, masters competent to teach them today. It is safer to be moderate in pranayama and ease off as soon as you experience negative side effects, such as headaches, irritability, or disorientation.

We our born with empty lungs. Our first act in this life is inhalation. Our last act at death is exhalation. For the yogi, every inhalation is a birth and every exhalation a death. Retention of full breath is suspension of life. Holding the lungs empty is suspension of death. Holding the breath is one of the easiest ways to stop the mind cold. However, mere lack of thoughts without expanded awareness is of no spiritual benefit. Depriving the brain and heart of oxygen can only be deleterious in the long run.

Hatha yogis are also the greatest skeptics, trusting concrete evidence and cold, dry logic more than speculative ideas or ever-shifting emotions.

The Saturn path loves silence, privacy, and seclusion. For guidance in the physical postures of Hatha Yoga, the Iyengar approach expresses the meticulous attention to detail necessary for proper practice of this path, although some of its adherents make the mistake of prescribing one "universal" set of postures for all people, rather than tailoring the practice to individual needs.

The Native American vision quest, a period of fasting, seclusion, and prayer in the wilderness, is another perfect example of Saturn's approach to spiritual unfoldment. Several Roman Catholic monastic orders also exemplify the Saturn path in their outer behavior, such as the austere Franciscans and silent Trappists. This path can also be called the Path of Silence, or the Path of the Hermit or Recluse. Those individuals who have an urge towards monastic life are often on the path of Saturn.

Each of the yogas has its own characteristic form of meditation. One Saturn meditation is just being empty, sitting very still and doing nothing, as in typical Zen practice. The meditator may just observe his breath, or count each stage of breathing in a very slow, deliberate manner.

The irony of the Saturn path is that it uses the body to transcend the body. Through assiduous attention to purifying the gross material sheath, the Hatha yogi becomes aware of the nonmaterial realm of pure spirit.

For all the yogas there are both a danger and an antidote for the danger. The general antidote is awareness of the validity of different paths for different people, and practice of the path most suited to one's unique personal spiritual nature. Since Saturn governs boundaries and the body, the greatest danger in the Saturn path is becoming mentally rigid or preoccupied with one's own body.

The physical body is the vehicle or mirror through which consciousness is able to shine. When the mirror is cleaned, consciousness is experienced more clearly. Many of the Ayurvedic practices of panchakarma are designed toward cleansing the physical vehicle for this purpose.

In addition to the wide range of Hatha Yoga practices, the whirling dervishes of the Sufi tradition and the ultrarunning disciples of Sri Chinmoy are classic examples of transcendence of the mind through the activity of the body. Indeed, most people have experienced this type of transcendence to some degree. It is the endorphin rush of the distance runner, the deep relaxation and sense of oneness one gets from exhausting physical activity.

The path of Hatha Yoga is all too often subtly undermined by teachers from other yogic paths. They treat it as a second class yoga, useful only as an adjunct therapy to one of the "major" yogas. However, for some it is a powerful path in its own right. *Better one's own path than the path of another. (Bhagavad Gita*, chapter 18, verse 47.)

All these classes with scantily clad men and women practicing yoga asanas in large groups are good for mere exercise. However, they are the antithesis of Hatha Yoga as a spiritual path. Hatha Yoga is meant to be practiced alone in a quiet and windless place. One must learn to do *asanas* (yoga postures) in a meditative way if one is on this path.

Individuals whose spiritual nature is governed by Saturn are often skeptical and cautious by nature. Their approach to the spiritual life needs to be concrete, practical, and tied to objective research and thought.

Saturnine spiritual beings have a tendency to turn their natural skepticism back on themselves, often as doubt or second-guessing. This is never a useful process and only deters their spiritual growth.

Saturnine beings always feel that they are in the world but not of it. They may have had these feelings even as children.

This is a path that grows stronger as a person gets older. Saturn governs old age.

Those on the path of Saturn will find spiritual nourishment in helping others through the "death and dying process." A dying person feels very comfortable around a Saturnine spiritual being. Hospice work and care for the dying are valuable forms of spiritual exercise for Saturnine beings as well. It enhances their feelings of silence and reclusiveness.

Ayurveda, Rolfing, or any other forms of holistic medicine directed at the body become a form of spiritual practice when focused on by a Saturnine spiritual being.

Nyaya Philosophy, with its emphasis on rational, logical thinking, is also a useful tool for enhancing a Saturnine being's spiritual life.

Life in ancient India was conducive to the practice of the reclusive aspect of this path. Modern life is in conflict with this path.

The path of Saturn is also the path of grief. Saturn is like a stern father who punishes the child who fails to stay with the present moment and longs for the past or the future. But a Saturnine spiritual being is also capable of transforming grief into spiritual insight.

Studying Western Philosophy is an appropriate spiritual exercise for those on the path of Saturn, as its emphasis on logic and reasoning appeals to the Saturnine mind.

Saturnine beings often have to deal with fear. In many instances this fear involves threats to their own boundaries, space, and privacy.

Saturnine beings love to simplify their life. They like to sweep the table clean and start over. Thus, when life's circumstances destroy everything they have created, they can actually feel a sense of elation.

Saturn brings a natural indolence to the individual's nature. If this indolence is not countered by physical discipline, it can create imbalances.

There is no such thing as a universal meditation; there are only styles of meditation. The Saturn style has an emphasis on simplicity, physical discipline, and (other than just sitting) doing very little in the name of meditation. Zen meditation is very Saturnine – one just sits, staring at a blank wall!

If one stays in silence too long, one will find it difficult to come out. One will postpone coming out, time and time again.

Saturnine beings are not always so sensitive to the subtleties of esoteric knowledge. They prefer a more grounded approach which they can concretely grasp.

Since the path of Saturn is somewhat in conflict with external duty and responsibility, people on this path need to find their version of a cave to which they can retreat periodically.

Saturn beings love pilgrimages to remote desert or mountain places where they can soak up silence in solitude.

Many of the early Christian "desert fathers" were on this path.

This is the path of the turtle. Because it seems so slow, it takes perseverance. But often it is the tortoise who wins the race, not the hare.

The physical body is the oldest and therefore the most developed of all the sheaths. Thus, it affords great protection to those on this path.

40

Some individuals on this path are temporarily overwhelmed by the grief it sometimes brings, but as they get older they value these experiences more than any other.

Those on the path of Saturn can be their own worst enemies when they turn their (normally) healthy skepticism towards themselves.

Individuals on this path need to learn to trust their natural skepticism. It serves them well in most cases.

Fundamentalism is a Saturnine trait. Its emphasis can be useful on this path as long as it is not projected onto others in a universal way.

Since this path requires considerable time, it confers importance on the science of longevity.

In today's world it may be difficult to do many of the purifications required in Hatha Yoga practice.

A Saturn person's need to establish clear personal boundaries can sometimes be a headache to others.

Saturnine spiritual beings can also be dogged in pursuing a subject. They won't let things go. This can be useful in their spiritual life, but not necessarily elsewhere.

In times of crisis or tragedy, you are blessed to have a spiritually evolved Saturnine person come into your life.

The American Indian spiritual tradition is basically Saturnine. Drumming, for example, grounds one in the physical. So does the harsh, austere life of the Hopi Indians.

Hatha Yogis often resort to more physical approaches to Self Realization, including the use of mind-altering drugs such as peyote or LSD. They employ these substances in a very disciplined way, if their spiritual nature is strong.

Beginners on the path of Saturn should focus on periodic pilgrimages to quiet, reclusive places where they can be in silent retreat for a few days, or even weeks, if time allows. Zen monasteries offer such services, but one can also rent a little cabin in the woods.

Additional Resources

Sudarshan Kriya, a unique breathing practice, as taught by Sri Sri Ravi Shankar's Art of Living foundation, as well as his "emptiness meditation", are Saturnine in nature. www.artofliving.org

Iyengar's form of Hatha Yoga is very Saturnine. It emphasizes precise technique as an important ingredient in bringing about proper purification.

Hatha Yoga by Ramacharaka is a useful book for helping Hatha Yogins simplify their life regimen.

The first 16 techniques of *Vigyana Bhairava Tantra* are Saturnine in nature.

VENUS

Venus governs our senses, sight, sound, touch, taste, smell. Her domain is our aesthetic sense, our sense of beauty, our appreciation of art, our romantic nature, romantic love, sexuality, and all aspects of the senses, sensuality.

Attributes

The enlightened use of the senses is for discovering the ultimate beauty of life without becoming addicted to sensory pleasures. Venus thrives on sweetness, positivity, and affirmation of all that is good and beautiful.

The senses naturally tend to move in the direction of greater charm or greater urgency, each moving in its own direction. A man who is listening to his wife, for example, may find that his sense of sight pulls his attention towards the window. Then his sense of smell may pull his attention towards the kitchen. Then his sense of taste may make him realize how hungry he is. Finally, he may develop an itch through his sense of touch and his attention goes to where the itch is. All this may take place within a few seconds.

For this reason some refer to the senses as monkeys running aimlessly here and there, but the senses are more like bees which move from flower to flower looking for more and more sweetness. In other words, it is the nature of the senses to expand outward looking for greater charm, happiness, power, and pleasure When this same tendency is directed inward, we have the makings of Raja Yoga, the spiritual path ruled by Venus.

Venus, like Jupiter, is a Minister in the planetary cabinet. However, she is a more active minister.

Conscience, which is linked to the conscious emotions, is ruled by Jupiter. The aspect of mind which organizes the input of the senses into output is ruled by Venus.

Venus seeks beauty in everything; therefore, she naturally engages in all the various forms of positive thinking. While some people see a rose and tend to focus on the thorns, a Venusian person will only focus on the beautiful rose petals. To paraphrase an old Indian story: Someone sees a dead dog in the road and recoils in horror; his Venusian companion says, "Oh, look at his beautiful white teeth." Or, "He had a good life and was a faithful companion to his master."

Venusian love is that keen edge of appreciation for the beloved which lets us see only his or her good points.

Venusian love is very idealistic. It is like the medieval knight courting the maiden in the queen's court.

Venusian love must be demonstrated through the senses for complete fulfillment.

Venus is so enamored of ideal beauty, proportion, and harmony that an essential part of her spiritual nature lies in seeking ideal love relationships. Unfortunately, some individuals fool themselves into believing that an ideal companion or mate is essential to their spiritual life. In reality they are just seeking another form of security. However, this can never be said of true Venusian spiritual beings. Their quest for an ideal mate is always in harmony with their highest nature and is always to be encouraged.

Venusian love is quite different from the love generated through the path of Bhakti Yoga. Venusian love needs to be demonstrated and enlivened through the senses. This is why the medieval courtship between knight and royal lady is so Venusian. It places great emphasis on the ideal love relationship and the demonstration of love in courtship and marriage. The love of the Bhakta is more inward; it is not so sensual.

Venus always seeks peace and compromise. For a Venusian soul, working for an organization which is trying to bring world peace becomes a form of spiritual exercise.

Venus thrives when she feels a sense of progress. This is reflected in the relationship of Venus to the arts. The aesthetic principle governed by Venus is the proper development and evolution of an artistic theme.

Venusian spiritual beings dislike being around negative persons, and for good reason. It is harmful to their spiritual evolution.

Things generally go smoothly and easily for a person when Venus has major significance in the esoteric star configurations.

"Fighting and making up" is not a relationship pattern suitable to a Venusian being. They like the last part but not the first.

If you constantly find fault with others, even with seemingly good cause, you probably are not a spiritual Venusian being.

Don't misunderstand me – everyone should engage in positive thinking, but Venusian beings will do it better and gain more from it spiritually than someone on another path to Self Realization. Their judgment as to what is positive thinking and how it is to be practiced will also be more idealistic.

A Venusian being sees what is unique and different about someone and honors those qualities.

Geomancy, the art of placing or designing buildings auspiciously, is the applied discipline ruled by Venus. It makes one's environment beautiful, pleasing, and harmonious.

Venus and Jupiter are both social beings, but Venus is sociable in a lighter, party-like, festive way. She is not so family- or church-oriented, either.

When Venus governs marriage for an individual, then he or she needs to feel courted even long after the hum-drum, day-to-day life of marriage has set in.

Lovingly contemplate the paintings of Matisse and you will gain an insight into the Venusian nature and how it expresses itself.

Symbol

 Divine spirit (circle) over matter (cross)

Gemstone

Venus is propitiated by wearing diamond or white sapphire. Some even suggest zircon as a substitute.

Sound

Venus's energetics can be felt by toning the vowel sound "a" as in "calm." When you chant this sound, you will sense that it is totally affirmative and life-supporting. The predominant vowel sound in the ancient

45

Sanskrit is "a." This is part of the reason people feel so good when listening to or chanting the Veda. When we see something beautiful, we naturally exclaim: "Aaah!"

Deity

Venus's deity is Lakshmi.

Light

Happy, positive, uplifting, nonjudgmental, creates beauty around them, projects a crystalline energy of purity and love.

Shadow

Critical of those who do not live up to her ideal, adheres to standards of beauty rigidly, judgmental. A dreamy sort of pseudo spiritual narcissism, where one is attached to positivity and avoids dealing with the sometimes harsh "realities" of daily life.

The Path Of The Senses
Raj Yoga

Venus governs the spiritual path of beauty and art. This path was called Raja Yoga in the ancient Vedic literature. "Raja" means kingly or royal. It was the path for kings and queens, who were (and in some cases still are) constantly surrounded by beautiful, lovely, inspiring objects. These objects can keep one rooted in materialism, or they can lift one to heaven; it all depends on the angle taken, on how the objects are used.

Kings and royalty are surrounded by material abundance, and it is important that they know how to use these sensory delights in a way that cultivates spiritual development. Thus, Raja Yoga is ideally tailored to affluent, cultured, artistic people. It teaches them how to turn the senses inward to achieve liberation, as well as outward for physical and aesthetic satisfaction.

Venus rules the senses, which naturally seek fields of greater and greater charm and beauty. For this reason, this spiritual path can also be called the path of beauty and art. In terms of spiritual practice, outer Raj Yoga involves refined art and music, and inner Raj Yoga involves refinement of the inner senses, primarily through simple sounds, or mantras, chosen to attune the individual to the cosmic harmony.

The mind may transcend through any of the senses, though a Raj Yogi's mind typically prefers one sense as his/her primary method.

The appreciation of art is a method that the mind can transcend through the sense of sight, accessing the universal aesthetic beauty experienced in nature or any aspect of visual life, such as the beauty of a sunset.

The Raj Yogi may also transcend through touch, or taste, or smell. Many of us have at one time or another had a meal that was so delicious it created a feeling of universal oneness, of connectedness with all of life, for example. This is not to imply that the Raj yogi can be a hedonist, indulging every sensory desire without restraint. On the contrary! Many people try to practice the outer behavioral disciplines of Raj Yoga without a simple inner technique of transcendence, putting the proverbial cart before the horse.

The senses draw the attention away from the bliss of Self awareness, so all the yogas require restraining the senses to some degree. Life in the body is not possible without some sensory experience. And the senses are unruly, like powerful wild horses pulling the mind from object to object. So how do you pursue Self-awareness while the senses pull you away? How do you minimize the struggle and maximize the bliss?

We have desires related to each of the eight levels of life. The planetary ruler of each yoga sublimates desires on both an outer and an inner dimension. The outer dimension is purification of action and surroundings to better reflect our infinite nature. The inner dimension is leading the attention away from outer objects of physical experience to subtler levels of inner spiritual experience.

Venus, the ruler of the senses, governs the desire for sensory pleasure. She can choose to either indulge in sensory pleasures, or sublimate those desires for suprasensory bliss, the calm and lasting inner fulfillment that is not associated with any specific experience. On an outer level, she avoids conflict by building an environment of beauty and harmony. On an inner level, she refines the senses to transcend the senses.

An ideal lover sees the beloved in the most appreciative terms. This keen edge of appreciation possesses the ability to ignore, or to be oblivious to, any defects in the other person and to see only their good points. He sees only the rose petals, not the thorns. This is why Raja Yoga necessarily includes positive thinking, with its affirmations, appreciations, and upbeat attitudes.

Maharishi Mahesh Yogi is a perfect example of a great modern Raj Yogi. His Transcendental Meditation (TM) Program and the TM- Siddhi Program are classic Raj Yoga at its best, naturally fluid and effortless. Transcendental Meditation®, as well as all mantra meditations, are Raj Yoga techniques in which the mind transcends through the sense of sound, using the sense of hearing. One experiences finer and finer states of a meaningless and harmonious sound to seduce the awareness away from the outer senses, until the sound disappears and the time-space boundaries of experience dissolve in the boundless bliss of the Self.

However, Raj Yogis who transcend through sound have also been known to transcend through music, such as a great symphony or even a highly-charged rock and roll song, or any type of music for that matter.

Just as Venus is the great peacemaker, the proper practice of Raj Yoga is a great antidote to stress and violence for both individual and society. As hundreds of scientific studies have shown, TM is very restful and uplifting to mind, body, and environment. It is also one of the easiest and safest paths for many diverse people to practice.

Maharishi Mahesh Yogi has established his organizations around the world in such a way that all the principles of Raja Yoga are paramount.

His organization exists primarily to spiritually empower the wealthy (The Raja Yogic Kings and Queens). If you doubt this, visit his Peace Palaces throughout the world, and see their emphasis on the creation of wealth, beauty, and harmony as the foundation for spiritual seeking and fulfillment.

Maharishi admitted as much in a number of public lectures and private meetings. In effect he has said, "I had to accept all the 'rag-tags' who came to me initially, but now I want to work primarily with the more creative, wealthy people. It is they who are most capable of helping the world, once they are properly empowered."

I (Edward) have no objection to this attitude and highlight it merely as an example of a pure Venusian approach.

Maharishi Mahesh Yogi has been equally strong on not allowing any negativity to exist within his organizations – another Raja Yogic principle. Such a policy is easily subject to abuse, and its emphasis is not always so useful for individuals or groups devoted to other spiritual approaches. For example, those on the path of Gyana Yoga need to ask tough questions which may appear negative on the surface but which play a vital role in the unfoldment of truth. Those on the path of Tantra need to be allowed to creatively rebel, even if the organizational structure shakes a bit. Those on the warrior path need to be allowed more independence in how they approach things, even when it appears to be a challenge to the organization.

Although the path of action (karma yoga) and the path of the Heart (bhakti yogi) are the most explicitly devotional, there is a devotional aspect of every path, even without belief in God. In Raj Yoga devotion is through appreciation of harmony and beauty. Maharishi gives the analogy of a great artist whose perfect sculpture adorns a public setting. Many people see the sculpture every day without giving it much notice, but one man is so captivated by it that he comes daily and is spellbound by its beauty. The art lover naturally dreams of meeting the great artist, and the artist is naturally delighted to meet the rare soul who really appreciates the beauty of his handiwork. In the same way, the Creator of the universe showers love and blessings on those who truly appreciate the infinite beauty of creation.

Even the movements seeking to bring world peace are, for Venusian individuals, sources of spiritual inspiration and exercise.

Affirmations are a form of spiritual exercise on the path of Raja Yoga.

Someone on the path of Raja Yoga will say, "Speak the sweet truth." Someone on the path of Gyana Yoga will feel that if he speaks truth, it will be sweet! What a difference of approach!

Venusian spiritual beings thrive in the feeling of tangible progress; otherwise, they doubt the efficacy of their path. Thus, they love to discuss their inner meditative experiences, and the flashier these experiences are, the better.

Sometimes marriage is a psychological letdown for a Venusian spiritual being. Marriage is a Saturnine institution; it involves bargaining over mutual needs, contractual duties, etc. Venus enjoys the courtship stage the most and is challenged to keep that sense of courtship within the confines of the traditional marriage.

The aspiration for a "soul mate" is legitimate for a Venusian spiritual being as long as she or he is not attached to the result.

A Venusian spiritual being has a natural ability to experience all of the arts in such a highly refined way, and thus can spiritually transcend through them. However, sometimes this natural gift must be developed and accentuated through reading books on this topic. The great artist Kandinsky wrote such a book, as have other artists, poets, and musicians. The Anthroposophical Society has also published a number of books relating to the spiritual in art.

Most people go to art museums or concerts as a form of recreation; for a Venusian being it is like going to a sacred site.

Although Venus governs all the senses, it governs most specifically the sense of taste. Thus, the culinary arts are under the domain of Venus. The sense of taste includes good taste in the arts.

Michelangelo was a great spiritual being and representative of the path of Venus. His works of art and sculpture bring alive the reality and beauty of the vital body in relation to the physical body.

A dolphin is a pure Venusian animal. Observe its movements, manners, and grace; you will get a feeling for this planetary energy.

The music of Johann Strauss and of Chopin are Venusian to the core.

The science of geomancy is the applied discipline that relates to Venus. This discipline teaches us how to organize our environment so that energy (*prana*, or *chi*) moves through it without obstruction. Those individuals who have Venus governing their spiritual nature are natural geomancers. Their refined sense of beauty tells them where to place objects and where to avoid placing them. For such people the practice of geomancy is a form of spiritual exercise.

Venus governs the second system of Indian Philosophy, Vaisheshika. This philosophy is a study of the uniqueness of each object, and uniqueness is a quality tied to the appreciation of beauty.

Vaisheshika philosophy is the equivalent of Western empirical science. It teaches us how to explore the nature of reality through the senses. Of course, these sciences have outstripped themselves. They are now beginning to discover that the physical reality perceived through the senses is intimately tied to mind.

Geomancy is the lazy Venusian's guide to enlightenment. This spiritual type loves to create an energetic "cocoon" and experience all the benefits of this harmonious environment without lifting a finger or thinking a thought!

Hypnosis is a legitimate part of the path of Venus, although self-hypnosis is less dangerous than the other kind.

A Venusian spiritual being should avoid negative environments like a zebra avoids lions!

Water is very soothing to a Venusian soul. So are plants and crystals.

The art of turning the senses inward to find fields of greater and greater charm is the path of Raja Yoga. Transcendental Meditation® is a perfect Raja Yogic path.

A Raja Yogic form of meditation should be simple, effortless, and natural. It should be done twice a day at a regular time and place. Why? First, because the vital body is drawn to do what is charming, and second, because it is enhanced by the regular alternation of rest and activity.

Raja Yogic groups and organizations have a difficult time distinguishing negative comments from constructive criticism. This tends to make them very insular.

Raja Yoga makes use of moral and ethical precepts, *asanas* and *pranayamas*, periodic withdrawal of the senses, and the three stages of meditation. These constitute the eight limbs of Yoga.

How one concentrates, contemplates, and gains transcendence (the last three limbs of Yoga) differs according to each spiritual path. The same can be said for many of the other limbs as well.

Many Raja Yogins can use the appreciation of art as a form of meditation, and this outward and informal form of meditation can be just as valuable as the more formal, inward stroke.

Inward meditation must always be balanced by dynamic activity in the practice of Raja Yoga. It is like dipping a cloth into dye (inward stroke) and hanging it out to dry in the sun (outward stroke). Some of the dye will remain in the cloth and some will be bleached out, but after repeating the process over and over again, eventually the cloth becomes colorfast.

Raja Yoga is not a universal path suitable to all; it is one of eight possible paths. I will admit, however, that it is one of the best yogas for beginners who are not certain of their own predominant strength of personality.

Patanjali's *Yoga Sutras* is both a handbook on yoga per se and a handbook on Raja Yoga. Carefully distinguish these two aspects when reading it; otherwise you will become confused.

The eight limbs of yoga should all be practiced together. *Samadhi* is that limb which can support all the other limbs, but few will be capable of samadhi without having experience in some of the other seven.

Siddhis are supernormal powers. Patanjali describes many of these. They can also be techniques of meditation for a Raja Yogin. Siddhis help stir the bliss which lies at the depths of existence, bringing liveliness to what often can seem to be a dry, flat experience. Each siddhi has a key word related to it which can be used as a form of meditation. As we begin to gain these powers, they become signposts of progress. The practice of siddhis gives a Raja Yogin that sense of progress that he/she so cherishes.

Siddhis can be dangerous if developed for their own sake.

Dream remembrance and analysis is a legitimate part of Raja Yoga.

Long exposure to mystical experiences and trance-like states is not harmful to a Raja Yogin; it is most useful – as long as dynamic activity is engaged in to balance these inward reveries.

A Raja Yogin lives for bliss, whether it is the inward bliss experienced in meditation, or the outward bliss of beauty in tangible form.

Raja Yogins should develop a rhythm to their meditation and action and never break that rhythm. The vital body thrives on it!

The paintings of Henri Matisse enliven Venusian qualities.

As a principle of art, Venus signifies the enticing development of a theme. Such work will display a sense of progress.

Strong Venusian spiritual beings who read my notes about this path will begin practicing it consciously, rather than in the subconscious way they formerly used their strength of personality (the senses).

Beginners in the path of Raja Yoga should make sure that their meditative practices are simple, effortless, and natural. Tapes related to self-hypnosis, guided meditation, or stress management can all be used as part of a meditative practice. Particularly useful will be sounds of the surf, or wind, or gentle flute music.

When a Venusian spiritual being does not enjoy meditation, it is because he is not following his artistic sense in choosing how and where to meditate each day. He is stuck in someone else's dogmatic assertions as to what he should be doing in the name of Raja Yoga. Of course, a certain amount of stress will have to be cleared out of the nervous system before any practice gives inner tranquility, but for a Venusian being, an artistic approach to meditation will be the best assurance of maximum stress release, as well as spiritual development.

Additional Resources

The Transcendental Meditation® organization exemplifies Raja Yoga. www.tm.org

There are a number of good books on the subject of Raja Yoga. Vivekananda's *Raja Yoga* is one. Ramacharaka's *A Series of Lessons in Raja Yoga* is another.

Ernest Holmes's *The Science of Mind* is a good book to help an individual discover the powers of mind, including positive thinking and imagining.

54

MARS

Mars governs our will. It is through a properly functioning will that we are able to achieve some goal or objective. It is our warrior nature that enables us to overcome all obstacles and to persevere. Mars is also about adventure, courage, subtle body energy channels and centers, and awakening kundalini, the primal fire at the base of the spine.

Attributes

Mars is the Commander-In-Chief of the planetary cabinet. He is skilled in motivating his subordinates to engage in dynamic action.

Others may set the objective of going to the moon, but it is the willful person who takes the practical steps to bring it about.

When Mars governs marriage, the person is quite willful in "going after" what they want from the relationship. They supervise things closely.

Mars governs Laya or Kundalini Yoga, the path of the spiritual warrior. The spiritual adventurer uses courage and discipline to conquer his primal drives and surrender to the Supreme Will.

Mars is drawn to the element of fire, whether it manifests as a warm, tropical climate, a warm room with a fireplace, or a career related to ovens and blast-furnaces, fire-fighting, or the conflagration of warfare.

Those with Mars governing their nature love adventure and risk-taking, no matter what Field of Living is involved.

Mars prefers to avoid the security that the world supposedly provides, because with security comes boredom.

Mars is masculine, like the Sun and Jupiter. It is pointedly assertive.

Mars governs the south, and since Mars also governs combat and enemies, it is considered wise not to have entrances facing south.

Mars can bring Type-A Behavior and even bouts of manic-depression.

Mars is liberal-minded, but also combative. He loves tests of will.

A Martian intellect is exacting and precise, particularly with respect to how a task is to be executed or completed.

Mars brings strength.

When a Martian personality is filled with anger, rage, or hate, say, "Yes," to him. Only later, when he has calmed down, should you try to reason with him. The same holds true for a solar personality.

Mars is a benefic or malefic, depending on the planet(s) it is associated with.

Symbol

 Drive (arrow) over divine spirit (circle)

Gemstone

Mars is propitiated by wearing red coral.

Sound

Tone the long "a" sound (as in "aim") and you will gain a feeling for the nature of this planet and its energetics.

Deity

Mars's deity is Kartikeya or Subramanya.

Light

Powerful focus, dynamism, fearlessness, courage, will power, indomitable spirit.

Shadow

Mars's shadow is anger, violence, impatience, frustration, overbearing ego.

The Path of the Spiritual Warrior
Laya Yoga/Shakti Kundalini

Laya Yoga, the Path of the Spiritual Warrior, also known as the path of Shakti Kundalini, is governed by Mars, and uses one's strength of will to facilitate awakening.

This path uses the subtle body, the chakras, and the awakening of the Kundalini energy. When the will is the predominant strength of personality, one naturally follows the spiritual path of the warrior.

Why do some people enjoy risky adventures like climbing mountains, racing cars, jumping off cliffs with a hang glider, or even going to war? These are outer expressions of Mars energy. He is the commander-in-chief of the planetary army, the adventurous risk-taker, the master tactician and technician. The spiritual warrior carries Mars' love of adventure into exploring uncharted realms of consciousness. Mars rules fire, both physical and spiritual. Kundalini Yoga awakens the primal fire at the base of the spine. The kundalini yogi uses this fire to transform carnal instincts into spiritual awareness, just as fire transforms dense, heavy matter into rarified gasses rising toward heaven.

Kundalini yoga usually begins with preparatory physical postures and pranayamas (breathing exercises) and strict control of diet and behavior. The goal is to awaken the dormant primal force in the sacrum and direct it upward through the central channel of the spine, called the *shushumna,* and pierce the various spiritual centers, or *chakras,* along the spine until it bursts into the top *chakra* in the head in a blaze of light and power. Since Mars is technically oriented, kundalini techniques can be very complex. *Bandhas* (postures that lock the breath in different energy centers), *mudras* (hand gestures) and concentration on the *chakras* with specific mantras and images are often used together.

Fast breath exercises are one way to fan the primal fire. Saturn likes slow, measured breathing. Mars prefers fast breathing (hyperventilation), possibly alternated with sudden, brief breath stops, just like a soldier who fights intensely, then suddenly stops to reassess the enemy, and jumps back into battle again and again.

The physical techniques of kundalini yoga are most effective if combined with inner practice, such as concentration on the chakras with appropriate mantras. An experienced guide is needed!

Lest we become enamored by the thrill potential of such practices, let us quote from Swami Rama's book, Choosing a Path:

"In my opinion these exercises are but preparation for awakening kundalini. I would like to warn students not to waste their time and energy in using physical techniques for awakening kundalini. I practiced these methods in my youth, but did not derive much spiritual benefit. Sometimes these techniques can injure the nervous system by disrupting the pranic vehicles. Excessive pranayamas and mudras can lead to ill health."

Mars rules the will, and willpower is the key to mastering the primal fire. This is certainly not the only path that can open the chakras. Others do so indirectly, however this path is the most direct and aggressive. The spiritual warrior seeks a high-voltage charge that will not quit, but he must have the discipline to control the wild physical and emotional blocks it can release. He must also be humble and unattached to any powers that may appear.

The primal fire flowing downward is experienced as sexual desire. Flowing upward it is experienced as higher awareness. In order to redirect the flow, celibacy is essential, at least during periods of intense practice. Of course, celibacy has always been a hot topic in religion. There are many simple guidelines that make celibacy easier, but most religions only teach outer control, not inner development, so celibacy remains a strain for most people. It is unnatural for most people to try to be celibate for a whole lifetime, but there are periods in everyone's life when it is necessary to abstain from sex, especially when learning to master the primal fire.

Sometimes the wise warrior uses stealth and surprise, rather than direct frontal attack. This side of the Mars path is seen in sorcery and shamanism. Carlos Castaneda's books are fascinating adventures in native Mexican shamanism, and excellent reading for all spiritual warriors.

In the great epics of India, the *Ramayana* and *Mahabharata,* battles are waged with powerful magic and illusion. Likewise, the spiritual warrior learns to play with perception and deception, manipulating reality to his will. And just as the good soldier serves a higher master, the spiritual warrior surrenders his own will to the cosmic will. This is the irony of the Martian path, one learns to assert his will only to surrender it!

Some excellent teachers, such as Paramahansa Yogananda, prescribe "kriya" techniques to raise the kundalini, but their gentle, soothing manner is really more akin to the Venusian path. The true Mars type shuns the soft and dreamy platitudes of Venus. He wants challenge, not rest and relaxation. Mars also loves variety and experimentation. His

59

path allows plunging into one technique after another, just as a recreational adventurer may go from skydiving to whitewater kayaking to hotdog skiing.

Another word of caution: the casual dabbler in Mars practices is like a reckless Rambo who charges into battle without a strategy. The successful spiritual warrior spends years in training and study. He knows his own strengths and weaknesses, as well as the enemy's. The real Mars yogi is the disciplined commander-in-chief of his own mind, body, and will, not a thrill-seeking soldier of fortune.

Although ritual is most closely associated with karma yoga, the path ruled by Jupiter, there is a ritual aspect of all paths. One powerful ritual used by some kundalini yogis and tantrics is the worship of Shri Yantra, which symbolizes the microcosmic/macro-cosmic union of male and female energies, and their transformation into spiritual power. Another Mars ritual with countless variations throughout the world is the fire sacrifice. The food and other gifts offered into the fire symbolize the ego we are burning in the fire of pure consciousness, freeing the spirit to rise to heaven.

Any technique that takes courage to confront problems directly also relates to Mars. Most of us live in denial on many levels. We shut out the memory of past trauma, especially emotional trauma of early childhood, when vulnerability and dependency are greatest. When a fragile ego or weak will is directly confronted with painful experience, whether through psychoanalysis, confrontational therapies, or accident, the trauma can be devastating. The same confrontation can be liberating to someone brave and strong enough to accept and rise above the pain. And what works for one person at one time may backfire for him at another time. So safety and success lie in knowing the appropriate technique for a given person, time, and place.

Where Mars addresses trauma with confrontation, other planets have other approaches. Venus, for example, dissolves it painlessly with sweetness and harmony, without ever confronting the problem directly.

Mars also governs conscious dying. He sees beyond the veil of death and transforms dying into rebirth. Many yogis are said to have mastered the art of conscious dying. One leaves the body on choice, not demand. One chooses to exit when the body has served its purpose in order to pursue new challenges outside the confines of the flesh.

Modern society tries to hide from death through a preoccupation with youth, sex, and staying busy. Contemplation of death is central to many Buddhist meditations. Although such practices strike many Westerners

60

as morbid, they can liberate the seeker from deep-seated fears and help one live fully in the moment, without regret for the past or anxiety for the future.

Mars gives courage to face death. The awareness that death could strike at any time helps us see beyond the limitations of life in the body. Similarly, Mars looks beyond the veil of waking consciousness into dreaming and sleeping. Saturn actually rules deep sleep, and Venus the dream state, but Mars penetrates the boundaries between states of consciousness and has the courage to face the deep emotional issues released by dreams.

The greatest warriors and athletes integrate rest and activity. They maintain relaxation while fully engaged in action, and alternate easily between sleep and wakefulness. Napoleon was known to sleep on the battlefield, and John F. Kennedy and Winston Churchill took catnaps at unconventional times. Restful alertness is a trait common to enlightened persons on all paths, but it is most dramatic on the dynamic path of Mars. Watch the equanimity and poise of Aaron Rodgers deftly throwing passes microseconds before brutally strong defenders smash him, and you will get an idea of the calm alertness needed by the kundalini yogi.

We have mentioned the risks of awakening the primal fire without adequate preparation. Another danger of the Mars path applies for people who should be on other paths. For them, excess emphasis on death can actually increase fatalism and passivity, rather than remove those traits.

Fatalism and passivity, so common in Buddhist and Hindu cultures, are the flip side of the imbalanced willfulness so common in the West. The Western conquest of nature through technology, an archetypical Mars syndrome, has precipitated environmental disaster. Fatalism and excess willfulness are just opposite faces of the same Mars disease: an egoic identification with the individual will, a result of nonsurrender to the Cosmic Will.

Such surrender is neither a mood of acceptance, nor the torpid passivity so common in disempowered people everywhere. It is attunement to Natural Law, which requires a full awakening of awareness, not a dull acquiescence. The soldier who sleeps through his duties is no better than one who charges into his personal battles while ignoring his commander. Enlightened surrender has two sides which may seem contradictory: taking full responsibility for one's own actions, and innocently allowing Divine grace to flow through you.

Since some Hatha Yogins have begun to use the term "Kundalini Yoga" to describe some aspects of Hatha Yoga, I prefer to use the term Laya Yoga to describe this spiritual path. However since the essence of this path is to enliven the kundalini energy in the subtle energy channels called *ida*, *pingala*, and *sushumna*, the other term is also appropriate. Just realize that the Hatha Yogic methods of rousing kundalini will be much more physically oriented than those used in Laya Yoga.

The will is responsible for finding willful and courageous means of achieving whatever goal, spiritual or otherwise, that the mind creates. Therefore, this is a path for a very independent type of spiritual seeker. Such a person needs a teacher who will honor his independent spirit.

People on this path love adventure and risk-taking. Since it's potentially dangerous to awaken and "ride" the kundalini serpent, they enjoy these risks and are usually capable of handling them.

Mars governs very subtle fire-element approaches to the spiritual life.

Laya Yogins enjoy experimenting with how they conduct their spiritual practices. They are also quite drawn to sexual activity (Mars). This gives them some affinity to Tantra. Nevertheless, they are Yogic practitioners and not Tantrics, and must learn not to confuse or mix the two approaches.

This is also called the Shamanic path.

The challenge of the spiritual warrior, especially female warriors, is learning when to show power and when to hide it. Don Juan, Carlos Castaneda's teacher, was a master at hiding his true nature except when he needed to display it. Why is this such an important issue? Someone constantly displaying a strong will is not looked upon favorably in a society seeking safety and security. Women in particular have been taught by our society to behave in ways that are not always compatible with being a warrior, and they may have a difficult time deciding when it is appropriate to let their inner strength of personality shine forth.

For all these reasons, I (Edward) often advise spiritual warriors to learn the delicate art of hiding their power in most social situations, and only displaying it when they need to protect some person or ideal.

Laya Yoga is a style of meditation where the focus is on the energy centers, or *chakras*, and the energy channels (nadis). These subtle channels and centers can be awakened through meditative techniques that use sound and light (either in combination, or exclusively).

<u>Chakra-enhancing Colors.</u> There is fairly universal agreement that the correspondence between colors and chakras is as follows.

Note: The following schemas, below, are presented visually so as to match the chakra order in the human system. Please view, read, intone and use in practice from the 1st chakra to the 7th chakra, or as you see fit, keeping this presentation in mind.

7th Chakra:	Purple
6th Chakra:	Indigo blue
5th Chakra:	Blue
4th Chakra:	Green
3rd Chakra:	Yellow
2nd Chakra:	Orange
1st Chakra:	Red

However, Orion experiences that the correspondence is this:

7th Chakra:	Yellow or Gold
6th Chakra:	Purple
5th Chakra:	Green
4th Chakra:	Blue
3rd Chakra:	Red
2nd Chakra:	Indigo blue
1st Chakra:	Orange

See which of these characterizations feels more resonant to you.

<u>Chakra-enhancing Sounds</u>

<u>Vowels.</u> There is less agreement as to which vowel sound relates to a particular chakra and for what purpose it is to be utilized. I (Edward) would suggest the following.

For a *sattwic* effect:

7th Chakra:	"au" as in "cow"	– Sun
6th Chakra:	"i" as in "ice"	– Moon
5th Chakra:	"a" as in "aim"	– Mars
4th Chakra:	"ee" as in "keep"	– Mercury
3rd Chakra:	"o" as in "comb"	– Jupiter
2nd Chakra:	"a" as in "calm"	– Venus
1st Chakra:	"u" as in "loop"	– Saturn

For a *rajasic* effect:

7th Chakra:	"u" as in "loop"	– Saturn
6th Chakra:	"o" as in "comb"	– Jupiter
5th Chakra:	"a" as in "aim"	– Mars
4th Chakra:	"au" as in "cow"	– Sun
3rd Chakra:	"a" as in "calm"	– Venus
2nd Chakra:	"ee" as in "keep"	– Mercury
1st Chakra:	"i" as in "ice"	– Moon

Note: Some sages have suggested that "a" (calm) is the second chakra sound and "ee" the third chakra sound if one is trying to create the psychological effects related to these chakras. I (Edward) tend to agree with this latter view.

For a *tamasic* effect:

7th Chakra:	"au" as in "cow"	– Sun
6th Chakra:	"ee" as in "keep"	– Mercury
5th Chakra:	"a" as in "aim"	– Mars
4th Chakra:	"i" as in "ice"	– Moon
3rd Chakra:	"a" as in "calm"	– Venus
2nd Chakra:	"o" as in "comb"	– Jupiter
1st Chakra:	"u" as in "loop"	– Saturn

Consonants.

Consonants. Consonants as they relate to the chakras are:

7th Chakra:	"aum" (not a pure consonant; a union of vowel and consonant)
6th Chakra:	"k"
5th Chakra:	"h"
4th Chakra:	"y"
3rd Chakra:	"r"
2nd Chakra:	"v"
1st Chakra:	"l"

Orion's version: Chakra-enhancing Colors and Sounds:

7th Chakra:	Sun:	Yellow	"au" as in "cow"
6th Chakra:	Jupiter:	Purple	"o" as in "comb"
5th Chakra:	Mercury:	Green	"ee" as in "keep"
4th Chakra:	Moon:	Blue	"i" as in "ice"
3rd Chakra:	Mars:	Red	"a" as in "aim"
2nd Chakra:	Venus:	Indigo Blue	"a" as in "calm"
1st Chakra:	Saturn:	Orange	"u" as in "loop"

No self-respecting Laya Yogin should accept these or other correspondences on faith, but should merely treat them as grist for the mill and as a basis for starting their own experimentation in Laya forms of meditation. Nevertheless, if they study the underlying paradigm of tamas, rajas, and sattwa and then experiment with these sounds in accordance with those principles, remarkable results may be achieved in body, mind, and spirit.

I hesitated a long time before deciding to bring out this previously hidden knowledge, respecting the adage, 'Don't cast pearls before swine.' But I reached the conclusion that the potential for abuse or neglect of this knowledge, and the karmic penalties stemming from either defect, is outweighed by its potential to heal all aspects of the body, mind, and spirit.

However, one word of caution: When toning, it is better to sequentially use all three sounds in relationship to a particular chakra than just one. This will help prevent non-alleviation or aggravation of a problem due to wrong judgment.

Each *tamasic* sound, especially when toned aloud, resonates in the chakra (and area of the body) to which that sound relates. For example, when you tone the "a" sound as in "aim", you can feel it resounding in the 5th chakra area. Or when you tone "ee" you can feel it in the head and within the 6th chakra.

The *rajasic* sounds have the capacity to enhance the psychological significations of each chakra.

The *sattwic* sounds enhance the spiritual energy of each chakra. Thus, a Gyana Yogi who wants to enhance his intellectual capacity for unfolding spirit can meditate with the "yem" or "yeng" sound.

The meaning and significations of each chakra are subject to some varying opinions. What is presented here are the unvarying seed ideas for each chakra:

7th Chakra: Beyond maya and illusion. Illumination. Inner Radiance.
6th Chakra: Wisdom, inspiration, insight, big picture awareness.
5th Chakra: Creative speech, articulation, analytical ability, clarity of mind, creative intelligence.
4th Chakra: Self-love as the basis for extending love unconditionally to others.
3rd Chakra: Courage, strength, and the ability to accomplish one's ends through a concentrated Will. Altruistic sociability based on inner confidence and the ability to influence other's minds.

2nd Chakra: Procreation, nerve vitality, and sociability which is tied to mutual likes and dislikes.

1st Chakra: Survival instinct, physical vitality, grounded-ness.

The applied discipline that also helps cultivate the spiritual life of a Laya Yogin is Gandharva Veda, or the study and use of primal sound. Present day Gandharva Veda can be used as a starting point in one's studies, but one should realize that it is no longer the true ancient discipline which once could produce rain, protect the innocent from harm, and bring totally life-supporting effects everywhere.

Sound and color can be combined in various types of meditations on each chakra. For example, one can think the sound "lum" visualized on a red-colored background at the area of the first chakra (perineum).

Many traditions offer techniques for harnessing and mobilizing the power of the will. Doing some routine each day with no utilitarian value – other than as an exercise of the will – can be very helpful for Laya Yogins in particular. For example, if you have no interest in gardening, you might buy a plant and tend it carefully each day for five minutes or so.

Since the enlivenment of the chakras through light and sound is by its very nature experimental, and not without risk, only adventurous individuals ruled by Mars will be drawn to such practices.

Not all prospective Laya Yogins are courageous enough to accept this path; they have become habituated to seeking security in all ways. At some point, however, they will get tired of the dull, hum-drum of life and will start taking reasonable risks again. Then their spirit will soar!

I try to be careful in how I offer spiritual advice to someone on the warrior path; I don't want to raise resistance in their strong-willed nature, nor threaten their independent approach to things.

Sometimes spiritual rebels will also take part in nationalistic rebellions. Their greatest spiritual growth, and even their enlightenment, may even take place in confinement!

As a spiritual warrior, a woman is often better off not taking a permanent marriage partner if he does not support her adventurous nature.

Additional Resources

Hatha Yoga: The Hidden Language by Swami Sivananda Radha is most appropriate for those who are on the path of Laya or Kundalini Yoga and want to learn Hatha Yoga in a way suitable to their own *sadhana*.

Kundalini Yoga by Swami Sivananda Radha is an excellent book on the practice of the warrior path. It highlights many additional ways to awaken and stabilize the chakras' energy in addition to light and sound techniques.

The Yoga of Power by Julius Evola fails to clearly distinguish Laya Yoga from Tantra; otherwise, it is an excellent book.

The Power of Will by Frank Haddock and *The Right Use of Will* by CeAnne DeRohan are two other books of merit for a Laya Yogin.

Laya Yoga by Goswami is an encyclopedic text on the practice of Laya Yoga.

EST (Erhard Seminars Training now known as Landmark Education offering the Landmark Forum and related programs) is a modern day example of a warrior regime for spiritual development. So is fire-walking, Outward Bound programs, and other regimes and practices that challenge the will.

Carlos Castaneda's books are excellent for telling stories with deep, hidden nuances, and even instructions which only a Laya Yogi will fully grasp. This is another meaning of the term "sorcerer".

THE MOON

The Moon governs the wisdom of the Heart, instant intuitional knowledge of anything, and devotion. Her domain is universal love, the nurturing love of the mother, home, and comfort. In its purest sense we experience the Moon as *agape* Love, universal Love for all things, motherly Love, nurturing energy, our right brain intuitive, creative nature.

Attributes

The Moon is the power of love, the infinite power of the Divine Mother to nourish and uplift all creation.

The Moon is the Queen of the planetary cabinet. As Queen, the Moon is coequal with her husband, the King (Sun). Together they are the paired principles of yin and yang, the feminine, receptive, and cool (yin) and masculine, directive, and hot (yang).

The Queen lovingly attends to the seed desires of the King to help instigate their fulfillment. And what does the King, the Sun, desire? To be seen. The Sun is our inner essence which wants to always be Present in our experience. So the Queen, our Heart, is in service to the King, our essence, by revealing Him, through Love and Devotion, as the truth of who we are as pure Presence.

The King's approach is more impersonal; the Queen's is more personal. She enlivens the Heart. She must see to it that the King's directives are personalized because while the King's directives apply to all, sometimes there are exceptions to the rule.

The Moon is the principle of mind, but more specifically right-brain mind, the feeling, intuitive, subtle, feminine aspect of the mind. Our definition of mind includes the whole realm of the subconscious, which we sometimes consciously access through deep emotions and feelings. This can manifest during hypnosis, dreams, or meditative reveries. It is for this reason that many have said that the doorway to Self Realization is through the feminine, the feminine aspect of mind, because she is this subtlest level of feeling that stands at the doorway to our true Self, beckoning us in with her expanded Heart.

She is the love of the Mother who welcomes us all with open arms, who wants us to be nourished and held and comforted in her loving arms.

The exterior, conscious mind is ruled by Jupiter. The interior, subconscious mind, the emotions, the feeling level, and the right-brain artistic, intuitive nature are ruled by the Moon.

The Moon governs that fine level of feeling within each individual which includes the whole range of the subconscious mind. The Moon governs the discipline of myth and archetype, which has the capacity to enliven this subconscious mind and bring it to conscious awareness.

The Moon represents pure intuition, the wisdom of the Heart. She is both the High Priestess and the loving mother who senses her children's needs before they do. Her light is the reflection of the pure consciousness of the Sun. As the Moon brings light to the darkness of the night, the energy of the Moon within reveals hidden truths in the collective subconscious.

Every person has an ideal abode. For a person ruled by the Moon in this arena, the ideal abode is a cool place near or on a large body of water. The Moon governs the northwest direction. She likes cool, moist places like Seattle or Portland.

Both the Sun and the Moon are sattwic planets. They tend to bring light, peace, and balance into our lives if they are strong.

Love is life's greatest healing balm. Those who love are tireless in their pursuit of lighting the flame of love in others.

Those whose spiritual nature is ruled by the Moon become Bhaktas. This is the path of the Heart and of devotional surrender.

Lunar spiritual beings are most drawn to Vedanta. They love to focus on the oneness of life. However, they first accept this oneness on faith, and only later actualize it through a long process of devotional surrender. This eventually leads to Vedantic insight and total enlightenment. Thus, in their own way they move through the three stages of spiritual development: 1) Religion; 2) Yogic Discipline; and 3) Wisdom.

It is best to propitiate the Moon on its own day, Monday, or on a new or full moon night.

Symbol

 Mind or evolving human spirit through receptivity (crescent)

Gemstone

The Moon loves the milky white color of pearl and moonstone. One propitiates her with these gems.

Sound

Tone the sound "i" as in "ice" to gain a feeling for this cold planet and its energetics.

Deity

The Moon's deity is Varuna, the water God.

Light

Unconditional Love, total acceptance, expanded Love, devotion, forgiveness, compassion, empathy.

Shadow

Codependence, control, smothering, manipulation.

The Path of the Heart and Devotion
Bhakti Yoga

Bhakti Yoga, the path of devotion, is the path of the Heart, which is ruled by the Moon. It involves intense, focused love for one particular manifestation, one particular person, or in some cases even a disembodied Presence, or one who is no longer appearing in a human body, such as Jesus or Krishna. This is the path of surrender to the divine in which the devotee surrenders his/her whole Being in Love and merges in the One Heart.

Often the devotee sings *bhajans* (devotional hymns) of love, adoration, to the beloved. The singing of bhajans can be both a path to awakening if done with one's full Heart, or it can be an expression of God's Love when it comes from the deepest level of pure awareness.

The Heart melts all separation between the devotee and the beloved. They may experience a oneness of Being. And through this oneness, there is an expansion of Love and experience of Oneness with All Being(s).

Bhaktas are often drawn to a personal relationship with a feminine aspect of the Divine; either the Divine Mother, the Blessed Mother, or a female deity like Lakshmi, Saraswati, or Durga. They are drawn to a highly personal, feeling-based relationship with their teacher. They are sometimes attracted to the traditional guru-disciple model where they can surrender to the Master and leave everything in his or her hands.

If a person's Bhakti nature is more masculine, he or she may not be so outwardly soft, gentle, and emotive, but more scholarly and wise and drawn to archetypal expressions of the divine such as deities and planets. An example of a person with a more masculine devotional nature was Joseph Campbell, who popularized myth and archetype.

A Bhakta could also be like a female tiger protecting her cubs. Love can be fierce and strong, as well as gentle and yielding.

The path of Bhakti has three major prongs:

- Personal prayer to the Creator – supplications to help all those in need or intense listening to bring the devotee into greater alignment with God's will.
- *Japa*, or repetition of the Divine Name – using a mantra or name with personal meaning which causes the heart to swell. Japa beads or rosary beads help remind the devotee to recite this name even

while active. Do not allow the practice to become mechanical. It must sink deep into the heart to be fully effective.
* *Bhajan* (devotional singing) and *Kirtan* (chanting the Divine names of God) either alone or in a group.

Ammachi is a great Bhakti Yogini. If you attend one of her gatherings, you will experience the power of bhajans and kirtan. Receiving her *darshan* is a classic example of a Bhakti spiritual practice.

Bhakti is the simplest path once one has enkindled a personal love relationship with the beloved Father-Mother God. Practice then goes by itself; love enkindles more love. You don't have to ask two lovers what they do to be in love with each other; they just bask in the mutual love their relationship inspires.

Once we have established a personal relationship with God, then no matter what comes into our life, we accept it as a loving gift from the Beloved. If suffering comes, we accept it as a great teaching from the Father-Mother. If pleasure comes, we accept it as well, but we don't cling to it. We are confident that no transient pleasure can rival the love of the Divine. We become contented with whatever comes into our life.

A bhakta (devotee) serves spontaneously from a heart overflowing with love. Saint Theresa of Avila and Saint Theresa of the Little Flower are two examples of western bhaktas. Anandamayi Ma and Mata Amritanandamayi (Amacchi) are examples of modern Indian bhaktas.

Bhaktas gravitate toward prayerful meditation or daily conversations with God as one's most intimate friend and companion. Since the Moon represents the mother principle, bhaktas tend to worship the Divine Mother more than the Divine Father.

Like Karma yogis, Bhaktas use ritual worship as an expression of their love, but their approach is less technical and more from the heart. Bhaktas become absorbed in simple recitation of the names of God. With extended conscious practice, that repetition becomes subconscious and instinctual. Their favorite prayers may become so automatic that they wake up in the morning feeling they have prayed all night, and go to bed at night feeling they have prayed all day. Their prayers and their actions are never selfish. They surrender all selfishness and delight in the joy of the beloved.

Bhaktas love devotional song and dance, and are often less restrained than their friends from other paths. The ecstatic displays of devotion by

St. John of the Cross, Ramakrishna, and countless other bhaktas have sometimes been a source of embarrassment to their more discrete and restrained friends.

Faith plays a larger role in the path of the heart than any of the other paths. Faith and love are natural for the Moon. "Love knows no reason," and the Moon is not afraid to love with abandon. She has no fear of love and needs no rationalization for caring and sharing. Feelings are primary, reasons and techniques, secondary. She may say, God is Love. Why debate the obvious? Why hide the truth of God's love behind a veneer of words? What you feel is real."

The Moon rules the oceans and the oceanic consciousness, where the collective unconsciousness of humanity meets the collective consciousness of divinity. This is the simplest path because there is no prescription except to flow with the simplest, deepest, purest feeling of love.

The Mother is always compassionate and receptive, but in that compassion she may discipline. Watch a mother tigress alternate tender affection with a stiff slap to her cubs. Although devotion is a simple path, it is not always easy. It requires total surrender!

The bhakti path uses feeling to transcend feeling. The purest form of devotion transcends devotion. Feeling implies duality, a separation of lover and beloved. Devotion implies a subject and object of devotion. The devotee's intense pangs of separation must be seen as a transitional phase. Her goal is to merge with the beloved, not perpetuating the agony of separation. This merger is at the deepest level of feeling, where differences dissolve in the unity of infinite love.

Dangers on this path are contrived emotionality and denial of common sense. As with all paths, one who is naturally suited for the path will be much more intuitively attuned to right practice than someone who artificially attempts to follow another's path.

How to enkindle this personal relationship with the Divine? Reading the autobiographies of great Bhakti saints, like Saint Theresa of Avila and Saint Theresa of the Little Flower, is one way. Storytelling is a personal way to enkindle the heart.

Studying the applied discipline known as myth and archetype is a more modern, Western way of practicing Bhakti, without all the guru-trappings. It will be much more appealing to some Bhaktas than the old ways.

Love seeks unity and oneness above all, and Vedanta is the system of thinking that emphasizes this reality. Bhaktas tend to be drawn to it. However, they tend to accept it on faith rather than playing with it intellectually.

Bhaktas are sometimes drawn to the Christian faith because of the strong heart quality personified by Christ and the Blessed Mother. Some aspects of Islam, such as the frequent bowing and total surrender, attract Bhaktas.

Enlightened humans have both sides of their nature, masculine and feminine, developed equally. Thus, male saints and teachers can also be suitable objects of devotion.

Bhakti Yoga entails personal service.

Even a spouse, a mother, or a child can be the object of devotion, although there may be drawbacks to such a practice.

Let the heart whisper what is the proper practice of Bhakti, without getting too caught in forms.

With most people the path of the Heart is also combined with greater intellectual activity, and takes the form of focus on the fundamental archetypes of creation and their expression.

The Bhakta finds his/her ultimate fulfillment in surrendering everything to God/Goddess.

Additional Resources

Bhakti Yoga by Swami Vivekananda gives useful advice to the Bhakta.

So does Swami Sivananda's book on Bhakti Yoga, part of his 23-volume set on the science of Yoga.

MERCURY

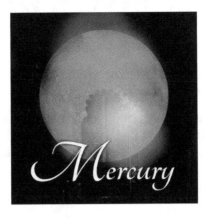

Mercury is our left-brain, analytical nature, which allows us to reason, and also to formulate language. Mercury is experienced as our intellect, that which distinguishes this from that. It is organizing power, creative intelligence, and detail orientation. It is that aspect of personality that has the capacity to stand back and watch and observe the play of life. It is the tool through which we make decisions and form judgments.

Attributes

Mercury is the Crown Prince in the planetary cabinet. When the intellect no longer acts solely in a discursive way, but also functions intuitively and with the deepest possible insight, it gains the entire world, including pure Spirit, represented by the Sun (King of the Cabinet). The Crown Prince becomes the King.

Mercury is an excellent communicator and rules all professions related to the rational mind and speech, and analytical faculties. It is personified as a thinker and knowledgeable in the field of mathematics. Mercury is also associated with barter, trade, and salsesmanship.

Mercury is flexible and adaptable. It tries to mold itself to the various people and situations it encounters. Mercury is serious among those who are serious; and jovial among those who are jovial.

The spiritual path of intellect is called Gyana Yoga in the ancient Veda. It is the way of pure knowledge, as exemplified by Thomas Aquinas, Rudolph Steiner, Paul Brunton, and J.R. Krishnamurti.

Like Saturn, Mercury is a skeptic and shuns blind faith. Saturn requires concrete facts and figures, and dominates modern materialistic education with its emphasis on form rather than substance. Mercury probes deeper, looking beyond the obvious surface values for subtler truths and higher causes. Saturn prefers silence, whereas Mercury delights in word play and excels in debate. The greatest of all gyanis, Adi Shankara, defeated the best-known philosophers of his time in great public debates with thousands in attendance.

Those ruled by this planet love playgrounds, gambling halls, museums, gardens, city walks, etc.

A Mercurial being seems cool and aloof to some people, because of its ability through the intellect to distance itself from what it observes. This is a strength, not a weakness; nevertheless, those who are incompatible with Mercury will view it as a fault.

The science of astrology is ruled by Mercury and Mercury alone.

Discursive reasoning can mature into intuition, which can, in turn, mature into insight.

Mercury is extremely introspective as when, for example, it knows how to look within through the question, "Who am I?" This question is the essence of the style of thinking called Yoga.

The intellect not only distinguishes the real from the illusory, it also makes meaningful distinctions within the ever-changing field of relativity.

This planet is like a playful 14-year-old.

Symbol

☿

Mind (crescent) poised over divine spirit (circle) and matter (cross)

Gemstone

Propitiate this planet by wearing an Emerald. Green Tourmaline and Peridot also may be helpful.

Sound

Tone the "e" sound as in "scream" to gain a feel for the energetics of this planet.

Deity

Mercury's deity is Maha Vishnu.

Light

Clear, discriminative, truth-oriented, open-minded, playful and creative.

Shadow

Critical, judgmental, argumentative, rigid.

Examples

Shankara, Ramana Maharishi, Papaji, Nisargadatta, Franklin Merrell-Wolff, Eckhart Tolle

The Path of the Intellect and Intellectual Discernment
Gyan Yoga

Gyan Yoga is the path of the intellect governed by Mercury. The intellect is different from the mind, though the two are related. The intellect is the discriminative aspect of mind which chooses, makes distinctions, and directs where we put our attention and focus.

Gyan Yoga involves making fine distinctions between what is real and what is unreal, between what changes, what comes and goes, and between what never changes, that part of experience that is the changeless witness, the subject or experiencer of all subject/object experience. The intellect has the ability to stand back from the daily events of life and dispassionately observe them. This process, if repeated on a regular basis, strips away the illusory from the Real.

As a surgeon wields a scalpel to cut away a malignant tumor, the Gyan yogi uses reason to cut away ignorance and misunderstanding. He knows that the ego's attachment to false belief is a veil to one's own true bliss, so he delights in exposing false conditioning and blind assumptions. The ego is revealed as a fiction, a nonentity which survives only as long as one clings to the belief that one is separate from the universal order. When the ego disappears, only the bliss of Self-awareness remains.

Mercury, the planet of transcendence, uses language to connect matter and spirit. He employs words to transcend words. As Lao Tsu said, "The Tao that can be put in words is not the Tao." The intellect cannot identify ultimate Truth. It can only cut away falsehood. The Sanskrit term is neti, neti, "not this, not this." One must examine carefully, time and time again, why one is not the body, the senses, the mind, the intellect, the will, the heart, or the integrating factor of personality. One cannot accept this on faith; one must find out the truth of it for oneself.

So the gyani questions everything, especially his own identity. He strips away false identification with his body, senses, mind, intellect, will, feelings, and finally, his sense of I-ness. Eventually he realizes the ultimate answer is beyond words, beyond conception, beyond thinking and feeling.

His mind does not spin in the attempt to discriminate. He just quietly and patiently observes the different levels of his personality, and the ego flees his inner gaze, trying to hide in the shadows of unexplored corners of consciousness. He silently witnesses his life, observing how the senses, mind, and feelings function. The analysis component is secondary to the witness value.

Nonjudgmental, neither active nor passive, just watching the mind churn, watching the ego judge and justify. Eventually the churning slows and stops, and the mind collapses into no-mind. Then ego disappears, for it can exist only in the active mind. The ego cannot live in silence. It cannot survive in light. It cannot breathe without duality, comparing self to nonself to justify its own fictitious existence.

Our beliefs shape our experience, not vice versa. We attract experiences based on our belief systems. If we believe the universe is impersonal matter controlled only by the mechanical laws of Newtonian physics, we experience tremendous worthlessness and despair. Our physical powers are so ridiculously puny and short-lived compared to the forces that create and destroy galaxies. However, if we deeply believe that all life is connected and we are an integral part of a cosmic plan that comprehends all the parts in the whole, then we find every moment of the day infinitely rich and joyous.

In Gyan Yoga, all statements that seek to portray truth are taken as merely grist for the mill. They are never accepted on faith. It may take many years to strip away all the false things we have been programmed to accept by our parents, family, teachers, etc. This is the first step of Gyan Yoga.

The second step is to slowly begin building our own version of reality, piece by piece.

The third step is to realize it is all just a game, and we can give it all up right now, or whenever we want to, and it totally doesn't matter. We can play actively in the drama of life, and know that our participation in it is of our own choosing. We are not that drama. We are immortal, unbounded consciousness, awareness, playing in the sea of consciousness with all these other aspects of my Self.

Shakespeare wrote, "Life is but a stage and we are the actors on it." Gyana teaches us not to be identified with any particular role we play as part of nature's master script. A part of this path is the perspective that everything is to a large extent pre-determined or destined. This perspective promotes the experience of witnessing all of life, like actors on a stage.

In other words, 'It was me, it was me, it was totally, totally me' is true and so is 'It wasn't me, I didn't do it.' See if you can grok that. This apparent dilemma, known popularly in philosophical circles as "the free will dilemma", automatically resolves itself when you see your Self fully as separate from this drama of life, and at the same time an integral part of all that is, like one wave on an ocean of consciousness flowing and dancing with all the other waves of the one Self, or Awareness. The 'It was totally me' perspective is the perspective of the ocean, the 'me' that is expanded awareness which is the essence of all. The 'It wasn't me, I didn't do it' perspective is the perspective of the individual wave, the perspective that separates itself, makes individual choices, and thinks it is the doer. The individual wave experiences that it is making choices and doing, but from the perspective of the ocean, which is a composite of all the individual waves, this seems like a very limited truth, as the powerful currents and influences of the whole ocean are always affecting the choices and experience of each individual wave.

No matter what our level of education, the intellect tries to maintain the ego's sense of separateness, by means of beliefs which we may be only dimly aware of. In ignorance the intellect is slave to the ego, working feverishly to maintain a sense of separateness. When serving a fragile ego, it is defensive, elusive, fragmented, and inconsistent. It either attacks blindly or retreats by avoiding the serious questions that might expose its master's mirage.

The gyani uses the intellect to cut the bondage to conditioned beliefs. By merely observing the ego's machinations without judgment, he frees himself from the painful belief in his own mortality and separateness.

Belief in God is not a prerequisite to any yoga, especially Hatha and Gyan Yoga. Gyanis of different cultures often see creation as a manifestation, an impersonal absolute, not a personal God who loves and protects all His or Her billions of children. Gyani philosophers typically say that it is simply the nature of the absolute to periodically manifest and periodically dissolve the manifestation. Some, like Adi Shankara, are also devotees of a personal God. Others, like many Buddhist and Jain philosophers, see no need to posit a personal God behind the creation. They may have very different views of the universe as either real or unreal. What they share in common is the primacy of Absolute Truth- that nondual Ultimate Reality which never changes and can never be put in words.

Self inquiry in its classic form is a Gyan Yogi path. Ramana Maharishi was one of the best-known Indian gyanis of the first half of this century. His main technique was simply asking "Who am I?"-the ultimate question every Gyani must ask himself intensely and repeatedly. The essence of Gyana Yoga is focusing attention on the "I" or "I am."

Sometimes this takes the form of a feeling deep within: "I am." At other times it may take the form of a question, like, "Who am I?" or "Who is this I?" If this "I am" were not a bridge to the eternal, focusing our attention there would have little value. However, because it is the great link between two worlds, its use as an object of inquiry yields enormous results.

Contemporary Gyanis include Jean Klein, and Ramesh Balsekar, a student of Shri Nisargadatta Maharaj. Other great Gyanis in recent Western tradition include Rudolph Steiner, Martin Heidegger, J.R. Krishnamurti, Rudolph Steiner, and Paul Brunton. Franklin Merrell-Wolff's expressions are a classic modern-day example of this way, as are Eckhart Tolle and David R. Hawkins.

Since Gyan is the path of the intellect, it is often thought of as the path for educated intellectuals. Actually, gyan requires no more formal education than any other path. Ramana Maharishi never finished high school, and Nisargadatta Maharaj had even less schooling. They also read little, but their brilliant reasoning disarmed the mightiest intellectuals.

Another common misconception about the path of the intellect is that it makes one dry and heartless. It is true that the intellect must be free of emotional bias to cut to the essence of any question, but right practice of any yoga only opens the heart. It is fashionable in some circles to drop platitudes about how all life is one, all people one, all paths one, etc. To the Gyani, such talk is nonsense. The clear intellect recognizes difference. To truly love and respect someone, honor his or her uniqueness. You only insult greatness by homogenizing it with mediocrity, like mixing clear water with mud.

Another common misconception about Gyan Yoga is that it is only for recluses, not active people in the world. This idea has two sources:

First, many people think that by realizing the ephemerality of worldly things, one must become disillusioned and disgusted with them and retreat to the forests. It is true that most saints pass through a "dark night of the soul" where ordinary concerns are seen as empty, but the inner vacuum left by disillusionment with finite dreams is just a preparation for spiritual fulfillment, a cleansing of the inner receptacle prior to full enlightenment. Periods of solitude may be a prerequisite for enlightenment, but most enlightened persons eventually return to an active life in society.

Second, Adi Shankara, the most influential philosopher in Indian history, has unfortunately been misinterpreted as a proponent of the

83

recluse way of life. There is a deep misconception in India that materiality and spirituality are opposed, that you have to renounce one for the other. People who are meant for a recluse way of life demonstrate tremendous emotional self-sufficiency from early childhood, shunning society for the joys of solitude and contemplation. They are a small percentage of the population. The wide-spread belief that one must renounce the world to find God has led millions of seekers into an abnormal reclusiveness which requires total denial of their desires. Such suffering in the name of enlightenment is like swimming in ice water to warm up.

All forms of yoga involve some restraint, but enlightenment comes from following one's own nature, not denying it. The important thing is to follow one's nature in the aspiration for the Supreme, and not squander this precious life in a preoccupation with petty wants.

This path often involves reading detailed philosophical treatises. Shankara's *Crest Jewel of Discrimination* is a classic example of this type of treatise, as is Descartes, and indeed many philosophical treatises.

Gyan Yoga is sometimes called "the pathless path" because its techniques are done equally well in activity as in silence. Why? Because the process of Gyan Yoga is the process of watching the whole functioning of the mind, intellect and ego through the observation of one's desires and negative and positive emotions.

The ego maintains its illusory identity through subterfuge, and this requires non-attention. When the mind turns on itself, remarkable things begin to happen; a slow, suffocation of the ego begins to take place merely through the power of attention. It is as simple as that.

Jyotish, or Vedic Astrology, is the applied discipline that brings the principles of Gyan Yoga into the practical lives of people. The function of the intellect is not only to help us discriminate between the real and the apparent, but also to organize knowledge in such a way as to create a perfect mirroring effect which throws us back onto the Self.

Put in still another way, only when we are able to see with complete clarity our eightfold spiritual nature, with all its strengths and weaknesses, can we then fully realize that we are not this play of life, this illusion, this Leela (the cosmic dance of the divine). It is all just a magnificent extraordinary play! Can you see it?

For some life may be a tragic drama. For some it is a romantic comedy. We all get to choose our favorite genre.

A Gyan Yogi must not rely on spiritual authority in any way. The intellect cannot function freely under such constraints. However, she/he must have great reverence for knowledge, for wisdom, wherever it is found.

In the path of Gyan Yoga, the individual stands back and objectively watches the functioning of his own ego. He begins to realize that the ego requires two basic things: security and power. The quest for security is nothing other than the need to maintain one's limited boundaries. The quest for power is the need to expand them. By observing these requirements of the ego, we begin to deprive it of the fuel it needs to survive.

The ego slowly evaporates when we watch it without any attachment or resistance.

The human being in ignorance is always running towards pleasure and away from pain. This psychological habit is the root cause of suffering.

For someone on the path of intellectual discernment, meditation is just as effective in activity as in silence, maybe even more so. Why? Because life is relationship, and in relationship we tend to see the workings of the ego more sharply. In relationship the human ego is very cunning; it is always seeking something from the other without having to give something of equal value in return.

The danger of Mercury's path is self-infatuation and indifference to others. Such defects are only indicative of incomplete insight into the path of Gyana. The true Gyani grows in love as he grows in discernment of how everyone and everything is unique and perfect in the context of the whole.

We are nothing objective or subjective. Anything which we perceive, we are not.

What separates a human from an animal is that the human knows that he knows. This realization is also an object of perception.

Sri Nisargadatta Maharaj stated, "Be happy with what you have and care not for what you don't have." This is the essence of the practice of Gyan Yoga.

The green light for coming back to the practice of Gyan is when we feel troubled in some way; when we have some problem, or when we are taking something too seriously. Then try to ferret out the core desire which you are clinging to which is causing the misery and suffering.

J.R. Krishnamurti said, "The solution to the problem lies in the problem itself." Don't try to escape from the problem; be with it!

A deep analysis of the nature of time, space, and causality is also important in the practice of Gyana Yoga. It helps to bring us to the state of non-duality if pursued with patience and vigor.

Too often sages fail to distinguish the knowledge of Gyana (the third step of the spiritual ladder) from the practice of Gyana Yoga. Certainly they are related, but they are also different. Gyana Yoga is only for one of eight people, whereas Gyana is for all advanced seekers.

Those on this path naturally tend to speak and write about spiritual things because when doing so, they deepen their understanding and experience.

An immature Gyani can sometimes tend to use his/her intellect as a club or razor in all his/her interactions; a mature Gyan only uses the intellect to help those who actively seek him/her out for advice and counsel. A mature Gyani does not need to "straighten out" the thinking of other people.

Gyana Yoga is a pathless path – all technique is eventually seen as workings of the ego. Wrestling consciously and directly with the ego is walking on the razor's edge.

Another spiritual exercise on this path is to take some principle of knowledge and contemplate it deeply. This process takes us in a vertical (deeper), rather than horizontal (sideways) direction. Deeper allows us to transcend thought. Sideways perpetuates more and more thoughts, examining all the nuances and logical ramifications of an idea.

Mercury is the energy that governs the path of the Gyana Yogi. Mercury is like a sprightly youth who likes to do everything quickly and easily. This is a tip as to how Mercurial spiritual beings might want to conduct themselves in the spiritual life, including their style of meditation.

Mercury has a refined sense of touch (just as Saturn has a refined sense of smell, Venus, taste; Jupiter, sight; and Mars, hearing). This sensitivity can be used in spiritual exercise in a variety of ways. For example, go to a botanical garden and put your hand over a number of different flowers... feel how they speak to you of their essence.

The laboriously written treatises of Western philosophy are quite different from the quick and facile metaphysical approaches of a Mercurial being. The former is ruled by Saturn.

Humor is a part of the path of Gyana, especially when a play on words is involved.

The deep, incisive questions and observations of the Gyani often disturb the more superficially minded.

The Gyana intuition is the result of refined thinking.

Claude Bolling's music, a combination of classical and jazz genres, is a good example of Mercurial music at its best. It can be listened to by those on the path of discernment as a form of spiritual exercise. Johann Sebastian Bach's music can be used in a similar way, although not with the same full effect – his path was not Mercurial, although it had a strong Mercurial influence.

Shankara's four qualifications for the study of Vendanta begin with discrimination between the real and the apparent. This in turn leads to detachment, the six virtues, and the passion for enlightenment. The process of simple observation is the catalyst for all further development. These qualifications are for all spiritual seekers, but they are the focal point for Gyana Yogis even at the beginning of their spiritual quest.

Paul Brunton stated, "Contemplation is attained when your thinking about a spiritual truth or about the spiritual goal, suddenly ceases of itself. The mind then enters into a perfectly still and rapt condition."

Modern education tends to distract and numb the intellect with a glut of unconnected information. Students become bored and frustrated because schools emphasize objective knowledge and suppress the need for subjective exploration into one's own consciousness. Today's education reinforces what Dr. Deepak Chopra aptly calls "the superstition of materialism," the belief that matter is primary and spirit is secondary or nonexistent.

A true education enhances discrimination between that which never changes, the Self, and the ever-changing mirage of phenomenal existence. It is more concerned with quality of consciousness than quantity of surface information.

Additional Resources

Commentaries on Living and *The First and Last Freedom* by J. Krishnamurti

Franklin Merrell-Wolff's, Eckhart Tolle's and, Ramana Maharishi's writings

JUPITER

Jupiter is the conscious mind that converts the raw data from the senses into coherent perceptions and conceptions. It represents the science of ritual which transforms ordinary activities into a yogic path to the divine, Karma Yoga, the path of selfless service. The Jupiterian mind is the power of conscience that whispers affirmatively or negatively to certain behaviors or activities. Jupiter is personified as the spiritual teacher, the Guru.

Jupiter is our sense of justice, fairness, of what is good, right, and moral.

Attributes

Jupiter governs the emotional or astral body, what Vedic teachers call manas, which is loosely translated as mind. It's just a part of what we ordinarily call mind-that part which forms simple concepts and has likes and dislikes.

His benevolent and expansive nature finds expression in love for family, community, and divinity.

Jupiter prospers when he performs action without attachment to the fruits, i.e., he serves out of love for humanity. He governs ethical behavior, action which helps others and upholds society.

Jupiter is the planet of abundance and good cheer. He maintains this good cheer by nonattachment to small personal desires, and derives joy from the happiness of others. Jupiter reveals to us how we can become exhausted if we remain attached to the fruit of desire and fail to sacrifice personal desires for the greater good of community or divinity.

This planet is very masculine; he loves outward expansion.

89

Along with Venus, Jupiter is the Minister in the planetary cabinet. However, Jupiter is the silent minister, while Venus is more active.

"Guru" is the Sanskrit name for Jupiter. The guru's Presence allows us to leave the surface of life and sink into its unbounded depths.

Jupiter loves abundance – not to hoard it, but to share it.

Jupiter relates to everything through conscious feeling.

Jupiter is scholarly by nature.

Jupiter is a natural benefic and great protector of those he shines upon. When he favorably influences the other star configurations, he can single-handedly wipe away a multitude of ills.

Jupiter is the significator of children. Children unconsciously demand selfless service and giving from parents. They are ideal candidates upon which to practice the spiritual path governed by Jupiter, the path of Karma Yoga!

Jupiter loves the affluent life of the city.

Jupiter's greatest attachments are sattwic ones: the guru, the church, the family, and the community.

Loyalty is a virtue highly esteemed by Jupiterian beings.

Jupiter likes to have a marriage partner with whom he can share every aspect of his life.

Religion is of great value to someone on a spiritual path ruled by Jupiter, but only if its rituals are lively and meaningful.

Symbol

♃ Mind (crescent) rising above the horizon of matter (cross)

Gemstone

Wearing golden topaz or yellow sapphire propitiates Jupiter.

Sound

Tone the "o" sound as in "phone" and you will feel the energetics of Jupiter. This sounds gathers things together; it brings about an embrace.

Deity

Indra is the deity associated with Jupiter.

Light

Wise, insightful, uplifting, able to see and share the big picture, generous, open, spiritual.

Shadow

Self-righteous, indignant, judgmental, critical. Attachments to philanthropy, tradition, religion, and morality. Jupiter's weak side is most evident as moral condescension toward others or condescension toward ourselves in the form of guilt and remorse. In either case, we are demeaning someone by measuring him or her against our own subjective moral standards.

The Path of Selfless Service
Karma Yoga

Karma Yoga, the path of the mind, is the path of selfless service, and is ruled by Jupiter.

Karma Yoga is the spiritual path of action. How do we turn a mundane activity into a meditative, spiritual one?

In the Bhagavad Gita, Lord Krishna instructed Arjuna in this path. He told Arjuna to act not for the fruit of action, but for the sake of the activity itself. Krishna says, "You have control over action alone, not over its fruits." Therefore, don't be attached to the goal of your activity, live for the activity itself. The Karma Yogi says his prayers and does his duty to the best of his ability, but does not worry about the outcome, as that is out of his hands. The archer can only pull back his bow, point his arrow, and release. He cannot control any sudden gusts of wind which may blow his arrow off target.

The central teaching of Karma yoga is nonattachment to the fruit of action. Jupiter is very generous and expansive. The essence of Karma yoga is selfless service, giving without thought for reward.

Why should we not be attached to the goal of our activity? When we observe life and our relationship to it, we will realize that we are not in charge of the fruit of our action anyway. So, why be attached to it? Success and failure depend more on support of Nature than our own actions. Furthermore, catastrophes can happen at any time. How many of those who died in the 9/11 tragedy thought they were in control of their lives? Probably most, if not all.

A Karma Yogin realizes that in giving, s/he receives much more than s/he has dispersed. This is a sattwic realization. Of course, if he gives in order to get back more than he gives, then he is still not acting in the full spirit of Karma Yoga.

The true Karma yogi enjoys giving without thought of reward. Unattached to his action and the fruit thereof, he gladly does his duty to God and man. On an outer level, that duty may be violent, as in the case of Arjuna and other warriors, or it may be nonviolent, as in the case of Gandhi and Martin Luther King. It may be religious work, Jupiter rules the priesthood and sacred ritual, or it may be secular, like the great philanthropist Andrew Carnegie who expresses Jupiter's generosity and abundance.

Karma means action, so this path involves the performing of rituals or actions in service to the guru. *Agni Homa* is a beautiful Vedic ritual in which participants offer gifts into a roaring fire while singing sacred songs or reciting mantras. Into the fire one offers/sacrifices precious objects like flowers, foods, and gems transforming them into gifts fit for the gods. This ritual is symbolic of Karma Yoga, through which we offer our every action into the fire of the Divine Life. This transformation through sacrifice is symbolic of the whole practice of karma yoga, governed by Jupiter, where we sacrifice our personal desires to the Divine.

Spirituality in all its myriad forms requires transcendence, and transcendence generally implies silent awareness. How is it possible to transcend in activity? It appears to be a contradiction in terms. Jupiter, the guru of the devas, knows that the infinite dynamism of creation coexists with the infinite silence of its Source. How does He incorporate silence into activity?

To answer this question, we must understand manas, the aspect of the mind which turns percept into concept and concept into action. It is distinguished from buddhi, the discriminative intellect. Buddhi is the seat of higher reason, the ability to probe to the core meaning beyond the surface value of words. When we say Einstein had a great mind, we are referring to his buddhi, not his manas. The vast majority of our thoughts occur in manas. For most of us, manas is forever spinning, blindly chasing desire, trying to relive the past or anticipate the future, and only dimly aware of the eternal beauty of the present.

Until we awaken our higher faculties, we live in a perpetual cycle of action, impression, and desire. We have no control over our actions because we have no control over our desires. As soon as we begin an action, a new wave of impressions floods the senses, and a new wave of desire wells up beyond control. Our daily lives become habitual repetitions of the same patterns of thought and action we've followed for years.

The first great faculty that makes humans so different from animals is the ability to use symbols and reflect on their own thoughts- qualities of manas. Animals have limited manas. Their physical and sensory capacities, ruled by Saturn and Venus, respectively, are more highly developed in some species than in humans, but even the most intelligent animals have limited ability to conceptualize, consider, and plan their actions. They act automatically and instinctively, with almost no self-awareness and little use of symbols. An animal learns to determine whether a rustling in the brush is friend or foe, predator or prey. But with the possible exception of the higher marine mammals, animal vocabularies and symbolic skills are minute compared to humans.

Humans, on the other hand, are richly endowed with symbolic skills they use in language, art, science, and technology. We could describe the whole of human civilization as symbol systems. By means of manas we translate our impressions (percepts) into symbols (conceptual expressions) and actions (physical expressions). Our symbols take on enormous power of their own. We fight wars over slogans, sacrifice health and wealth in the pursuit of ideals, and organize our societies around the shared symbols embodied in our political, educational, and economic institutions.

Why are we caught in this cycle of desire, action, and impression?

Why is most of our mental energy wasted dwelling on the past and future, barely tasting the eternal glory of the present? Because of desire, say the sages. Not that desire is bad. Life is not possible without desire. Suffering and imbalance arise only when we let desires overshadow our inner fullness and our intimate connection with all life.

The Karma yogi takes control of the cycle at the only point where it can be managed, the gap between impression and desire. Manas organizes the raw data of sensory impressions into meaningful images and abstracts them into symbols (words, pictures, music, etc.). The sensate mind of animals has minimal symbolic skills. Symbolic skills give us the power to rise above our lower passions and selfish tendencies. The most obvious human symbolic skill, language, opens up boundless possibilities related to Jupiter. It lets us learn ethical standards to guide our thoughts and actions. It preserves knowledge from generation to generation. It lets us share our joys and sorrows and celebrate together to strength our common bonds.

One type of Karma yoga is sacred ritual, symbolic action to elevate the mundane to the divine and express appreciation to the higher powers of Nature. It purifies the whole cycle of action-impression- conception-desire. Ritual requires sacrifice. Selfish desires are sacrificed for a higher purpose, such as service to God, country, alma mater, or the impoverished.

For many people, ritual has the dual effect of elevating the worshipper's awareness and winning support of the supersensible beings operating behind the visible world. Just as great heads of state are receptive to citizens who approach them with the proper protocol and respect, the higher powers of nature listen patiently to people who honor them in ritual, especially heartfelt rituals and ancient rituals which have survived the test of time. Although the major world religions have lost most of their knowledge of transcendence, they have all maintained certain ceremonies which continue to have power, especially for those who have done the inner work necessary to appreciate their significance.

There are many levels of ritual. Suffice it to say that empty ritual, without feeling or understanding, is of little value. Heartfelt ritual, with rich symbology and understanding, stimulates the deepest wellsprings of life and thrills the higher powers of nature, who reward the worshipper generously for his offerings.

With regular practice ritual becomes habitual. We cultivate the habit of offering all our actions to the divine. All our thoughts become prayers, our words blessings, our actions services. Then action, which has been a means of bondage, becomes a means of liberation.

Jupiter rules scripture and gurus. Karma yogis know from the study of scripture and the example of great sages that silence and activity are two sides of the same eternal Reality. The Karma yogi follows the example of great saints, scholars, and philanthropists, and conducts his daily life in a manner that reminds him of the Almighty. He treats all life with reverence, as even the most wretched of sinners is a perfect expression of cosmic order. He is also inspired to visit sacred sites where he can meditate or worship in an environment enriched by enlightened beings.

Although the Karma yogi may find deep rest and relaxation in silent meditation, his primary vehicle for evolution is selfless service. As his mind develops, he becomes increasingly sensitive to the needs of others and his own unique gifts for helping them. Rather than acting out of some onerous sense of duty, he learns to respond spontaneously, intuitively, and joyously. He learns to rest in activity. As he becomes attuned to nature, his thoughts and actions become superfluid, and deep knots of frustration and conflict evaporate. He discovers through experience something psychologists are only beginning to understand, that all neuroses are rooted in attachment.

Releasing our surface attachments removes hidden obstacles to fulfillment of our deeper desires, those inspired by cosmic intelligence.

The Karma yogi gains maximum benefit from meditation techniques he can use in activity, followed by a brief period of silence to complete the cycle of rest and activity. The late great Kashmiri saint, Lakshman Jee (a.k.a. Lakshman Joo) , said that an active meditation is a thousand times more powerful than a silent one for the Karma yogi. Again, a word of caution for yogis of other paths, trying to remember a mantra in activity may just divide the mind. An exception applies to people on the path of the heart, where remembrance of the names of God becomes spontaneous and automatic.

95

Jupiter also governs morality. As a practical teacher, he knows that most people have neither the time nor the inclination to spend all day in worship. They need guidance in daily life to prevent gross mistakes that could derail their evolution or disrupt society.

Morality is often confused with spirituality. All the universal principles of moral behavior are necessary to prevent physical, emotional, and spiritual damage. But spirituality is transcendental, not behavioral.

The ash heaps of history are full of seekers who fell prey to temptation and violated basic standards of morality. If we practice surface morality, without inner inspiration, we suffer a constant tension between what we want to do and what we ought to do. Indulge your desires, and remain their slave. Suppress them, and suffer all kinds of frustration. Either way, you are divided. So what do we do? If we are yogis, we are very selective in the desires we follow. We don't deny desire; we learn to redirect the energy of life-damaging tendencies and purify our minds and bodies so that all our desires become spontaneously life-supporting.

Inner practice does not relieve us of the need to watch our outer behavior, but it facilitates the process enormously. Even a good night's sleep makes it much easier to speak and act rightly.

No matter what our path, as our consciousness develops, our desires flow more and more with the stream of evolution and gradually gain the infinite power of Nature for their fruition. The gap between our "want's" and "should's" disappears as individual life joins the current of cosmic life. Paradoxically, in surrendering our surface desires, we find fulfillment of all our needs, physical, mental, and spiritual.

There is one danger in all spiritual practices - attachment to the path to the extent that one loses sight of the goal. This attachment takes a different form in each of the great paths. In Karma yoga, it may take the form of attachment to one's own guru or religion, or a pompous piety and surface morality. The antidote is understanding how different forms of action, good and bad, are a necessary part of the cosmic plan. Saints would never realize their potential for saintliness without sinners to test them!

The experience of *darshan*, of sitting in the presence of the teacher/guru, someone who is more spiritually advanced or who embodies a higher state of consciousness, facilitates the mind surrendering to its source. This is the action of the mind, an aspect of Karma Yoga.

Karma Yoga involves a process orientation, as opposed to a goal orientation. It also involves making activities which may seem ordinary to most people sacred or special in some way.

The Karma Yogi likes to create events or celebrations. One Karma Yogi I know films many activities of everyday life, making them special or sacred in doing so.

Although the Karma Yogi may have one primary teacher, or *guru*, he/she will ultimately recognize the *satguru* in many or all forms.

Jupiterian beings are known for their depth of intuitive insight, for their wisdom.

This path is for the householder who loves dynamic activity in the world.

A time comes in the practice of Karma Yoga when one realizes that one is not even the giver, but merely the vessel through which the abundance of life flows.

Life is nothing more than a mutual sacrifice between gods and people. The gods sacrifice their unboundedness to create and maintain the boundaries of the world, and humans sacrifice the boundaries of their egos in offering to the gods.

When we see a beautiful fawn born from her mother's womb and then immediately killed and eaten by a predator, we are horrified until it dawns on us that life is filled with sacrifice at every moment.

The Sanskrit name for Jupiter is "Guru," the spiritual teacher who dedicates his life to helping others. A Karma Yogin is meant to act like a priest who makes every action a meaningful, ritualistic offering. S/he makes every action in the world, no matter how trivial or mundane, an offering to the Divine.

The ego lives to grow and expand. When we choose to live for the purpose of giving (more than we receive), the ego shrinks down to nothing. In a beautiful Native American tradition, at the end of each year the leaders of the tribe gave away everything that they had to others. This was deemed a sign of greatness; a great man engages in selfless service and giving to the community. By doing so, he also demonstrates his confidence that he can easily replenish his wealth.

A Karma Yogin makes his/her output (action) sacred by offering it up to others. S/He also sees his inputs (everything s/he experiences) as omens/lessons from Mother Nature. Nothing that happens to him is without significance. A crow flying overhead in a certain direction will be

97

meaningful, not just a chance event. A telephone call at a certain time will signify something to him. He doesn't have to look for meaning; it comes to him intuitively.

When the input is sacred and the output is sacred, then the sacred hoop of the American Indians is complete. Life now revolves in a circle of sacredness.

The path of Jupiter is the path of *satsang*, sitting with the guru and imbibing his sattwic radiance (*darshan*). For the more immature seeker, the guru must be a living human being; for the more mature seeker, the inner guru becomes the guide.

The inner guru can be Mother Nature herself, who constantly whispers advice through omens which come to us each day by way of the senses. It can also be our own still small voice of conscience, which whispers, "Yes," and "No," to our various choices. One is in macrocosmic form, the other in microcosmic form.

Satsang includes the guru's establishment of spiritual and religious community, so that fellow seekers can inspire and serve one another. Jupiter loves fellowship in community (a.k.a. *sangha*).

The path of Jupiter is the path of religion. Not dead religion with dead rituals, but religion which is truly celebrative for the participants. For a true Karma Yogin, getting together with a few close friends to share in the celebration of family and community life can be a more meaningful religious experience than attending church out of mere habit.

Religion and ritual go hand in hand as aspects of Karma Yoga. Ritual supports Karma Yoga by helping to ensure that any activity, no matter how mundane, is performed in a sacred manner. For example, if you don't like doing dishes, then perform this task in a ritualistic manner and see the change in your attitude. Any action we want to offer to the Divine should be done impeccably; ritual helps put us in the proper frame of mind.

For a beginner in Karma Yoga, it is good to make a list of your major activities for the day when you first get up. Then offer them up to God in a very heartfelt way. Also make a resolution to stay in the spirit of Karma Yoga throughout the day while performing each activity.

A distortion of the true meaning of Karma Yoga found at some ashrams is to require disciples and guests to perform seva as part of community life. However, Jupiter thrives in forms of selfless service which he himself feels motivated to do, not activities dictated by others. All forms of seva, to be truly effective, should be strictly voluntary and self-chosen.

It is an art to know whom to serve and to what extent. After all, people exist who merely want to take advantage of others. It is not always valuable to serve such people in the way they ask. One's touchstone in these situations should be: Does this form of service give me a sense of expansiveness, joy and celebration, or am I merely motivated by some sense of pressure, duty, or obligation? If your motivations fall into the second group, refrain from acting.

Additional Resources

Maharishi Mahesh Yogi, *Bhagavad-Gita: A New Translation and Commentary, Chapters 1-6*

Swami Sivananda

THE SUN

The Sun we experience as our self-confidence, our self-esteem, our inner essence, pure awareness. The Sun is the King of the planetary family, representing pure awareness, essence, as well as our experience of Self, and of individual self, ego.

Attributes

The Sun represents the Fullness of life from which all life springs, and to which all life returns. This fullness of life is the fullness of Spirit, our inner essence.

The Sun represents the highest in all fields - trees among plants, gold among metals, kings among people. The tree gives fruit and shade to all, good and bad, rich and poor, happy and sad. Gold represents the Sun's generosity, liberality, and benevolence, ever free of rust. The King integrates and balances the various factions in his kingdom.

The Sun is the pivot of the solar system integrating all the various philosophies and points of view without being pulled into any of them, just as the Sun remains firm relative to all the planets that revolve around Him.

The Sun consults the specialists but is more concerned with the whole than the parts, with the big picture rather than the details. He shines best as the prime mover of a community, sometimes as a visible leader, and sometimes as a silent catalyst.

The Sun wants 200 percent of life – 100 percent spiritual (unmanifest) and 100 percent physical (manifest). He likes to lead in both arenas as well.

The Sun likes to display itself, just as the physical Sun marches across the sky from early morning to late night, radiating its majesty.

The Sun is a general significator for pure Spirit and is primarily located in our 7th chakra.

The Sun is the integrating factor within the personality. It gives us a sense of wholeness which in turn, becomes a center around which all the other aspects of personality group themselves – just as the Sun on the macrocosmic level is the focal point around which all the planets revolve. In other words, the Sun gives us our sense of individuality or fullness of self.

The individual is a microcosm of the universe. The universality within the personality is provided by the Sun; the diversity is provided by the other planets.

The Sun is always impersonal, universal, and liberal in its approach to any subject.

When the Sun governs a particular Field of Living, he represents leadership.

Those ruled by the Sun in spiritual life are not shy about their spiritual life, even though they may be shy in other ways. They will take charge of their own spiritual evolution, like a king taking charge of his kingdom.

The Sun has great confidence in itself. He is very charismatic and loves to shine in front of others. Many actors and actresses are under the Sun's influence, whether in their career nature, play nature, or spiritual nature.

The Sun takes an integral approach to everything it does, which means it is all-encompassing and holistic, taking in all sides of an issue.

Like a hereditary king who naturally rules his kingdom, the Sun automatically knows without knowing why he knows.

The Sun is seldom influenced by others in making his decision, or if he is, it is the collective influence of all the key players which he takes into consideration.

The Sun is more of a behind-the-scenes catalyst for action than the immediate instigator or agent of action. These latter roles belong to other members of the planetary cabinet. This is why the king sits without moving, while the battle waged by his generals rages around him.

The aspect of personality ruled by the Sun is the one that integrates the various aspects of personality into a sense of wholeness. For lack of a better term, we can call it the ego principle – divorced, however, of its negative connotations.

Don't make the mistake of thinking that all these significations of the Sun apply to you because you have the Sun placed somewhere in your horoscope. The Sun can only govern one of your eight Fields of Living. For you it might be spiritual life; for the next person it might be relationships or mental health.

All the significations of the Sun, divorced of their earthly connotations, describe the spiritual beings known as the Seraphim.

Symbol

 Divine spirit (circle) surrounding the seed of potential.

Gemstone

The Sun is propitiated by wearing red ruby or garnet.

Sound

Tone the sound "au" as in "meow" and you will gain a feel for the nature of the Sun and its energetics.

Deity

The Sun's deity is Agni.

Light

Radiant, self-confident, leadership qualities, inner strength.

Shadow

Conceit, self-centeredness, insensitivity, arrogance. The Achilles heel of the Sun is pride and concern over his reputation.

The Integral Path
Surya Yoga

Surya Yoga, the spiritual path of the Sun, is known as the integral path in that a Surya Yogi will explore many or all of the paths, integrating them all or deriving benefit from each, transcending through each but not alighting on any one for very long. The Surya Yogi is like a honey bee that goes from flower to flower, gathering nectar from each but never sucking any one completely dry.

Those whose spiritual nature is ruled by the Sun tend to naturally enjoy all of the approaches to Self Realization. All others are meant to follow one specific approach. They have a very liberal approach to spiritual development. They like to experiment with all the approaches and even combine them in different and creative ways. The Surya yogi knows what practice is appropriate at what time, just as the Sun defines the time of day. He does not get stuck in techniques or limiting beliefs. Diversity is not possible without unity, and the Surya yogi always sees unity as primary.

Those who follow the spiritual path of the Sun follow the integral path that unites Heart, Mind, and Will in service to the Supreme. The Sun represents all paths and no path, for the King supports all and listens to all, but follows his own inner guide rather than another person's path.

Surya Yoga is also known as the pathless path in that it recognizes that there is no one path. In fact, there is no path at all, standing apart from all paths and realizing the truth of who one is, separate from all practices.

Just as the physical Sun in our universe binds together all the planets, those whose spiritual nature is ruled by the Sun are most likely to appreciate all of the different spiritual paths.

The Sun is the king of the planetary family. The king is independent by nature; she or he has a natural tendency to follow her or his own inner guidance in everything they do. The same holds true for those who are ruled by the Sun in their spiritual life. They must trust that they know best even when they aren't sure why they have this inner sense of confident knowingness.

A person who wants to be his own authority often feels like he is out on a limb with nothing to lean on. She may think, "Why can't I be like other people and have some authority to rely on?" Only when she has had her solar nature confirmed can she realize that she cannot have both security

104

and independence. When she realizes this, she will always choose independence; her kingly nature allows no other choice.

The axiom "Don't be a jack of all trades and master of none" does not properly apply to a Surya Yogin, who is meant to go into the spiritual marketplace and buy all the different brands and experiment with them. The joy of the Sun is the integration of many diverse approaches to the spiritual life.

Nevertheless, the Sun should not get caught in any one approach at the expense of an integral one. This would display spiritual weakness.

If there are six major yogic approaches, how is the Sun to integrate them all, and on what schedule? If you ponder this, you will come to understand why the Sun needs to be her own spiritual authority. What outside authority could fix an adequate schedule for experimenting with all the other various Yogas: Hatha, Raja, Karma, Gyana, Laya, and Bhakti.

To simplify things, a Surya Yogin tends to stay focused primarily on the integral development of heart, mind and will through Bhakti Yoga, then Gyana Yoga and then Karma Yoga. But she may also give attention to the other three – Laya, Hatha, and Raj.

The Long Path of spiritual development emphasizes both our ignorance and the long road to enlightenment. The Short Path emphasizes our spiritual kingship and the fact that we are already That! Solar Yogis favor this approach, and when more mature, give a lot of emphasis to it.

If you try to look directly at the Sun, it blinds you and you get disoriented. The solar path is likewise paradoxical and is often called "the pathless path." If one is the wholeness of consciousness, where is there to go, and who is travelling there?

For some period of time (one day, week, or month) the Solar type may cultivate his heart, then switch to the mind and spiritual study, and then to cultivating the will. At other times he or she may play with all three simultaneously. There can be no set way for practicing this Yoga.

The Sun governs the applied discipline of community building, especially spiritually-based community building. Thus, the Sun's spiritual life is enhanced in spiritual community, but often only if he or she has a leadership role in the community. Then his or her spiritual nature can fully exercise itself.

Surya Yogins radiate their teaching by their very presence or by *shaktipat*, not so much by what they say. The same is true of the physical sun – just sit in its rays and you will feel better, as long as you don't overdo it.

The leadership of a solar being need not be obvious or external; it may consist of being a behind-the-scenes catalyst for some needed process or event. The Solar spiritual leader teaches mostly by example.

Solar types can be very charismatic; they can be accepted as gurus by the "true believer" before they are able to actually fulfill this role. The strength of their spiritual natures will determine how they deal with this temptation.

The Sun is avant-garde in everything she or he does, including spiritual ventures. Thus their play is often misunderstood and may be labeled as "meaningless" or too "far-out." A solar being is always 50-100 years ahead of his or her time, sometimes even centuries ahead.

While the gyani finds the Self through negation, stripping away all that he is not, the Surya yogi is more likely to use affirmation. He accepts everything as himself - good and bad, absolute and relative, self and nonself. The Surya yogi has the most direct relationship to the Infinite, without dependence on techniques. He may practice any spiritual technique, especially techniques of radiating the inner light. But his real practice transcends techniques and continues twenty-four hours a day. Any meditation practice which is not integrated into activity is not integral yoga. Integral yoga integrates waking, dreaming, and sleeping in an unbroken continuum of unbounded pure consciousness.

The danger of the solar path is pride, preoccupation with finite self and how one appears to others. Solar yogis with inadequate understanding of the ego's artifices and people not suited for this path may only inflate their egos by trying to follow it. For this reason, it is advisable for seekers on this path to combine negation and affirmation: negation of the small self, identified with the individual mind-body, and affirmation of the eternal, immortal Self of all beings.

Ramakrishna was a great Surya Yogin, as was Shivananda who founded the Divine Life Society in Rishikesh, India. Another outstanding Surya yogi is Swami Brahmananda Saraswati, Maharishi Mahesh Yogi's beloved "Guru Dev," who held the post of Shankaracharya of the North in India, the most prestigious religious position in Northern India. As a boy of nine he fiercely asserted his independence and ran away from home in search of God. For sixty years he lived in remote forests and mountains until he reluctantly accepted the post of Shankaracharya. This description of him by Maharishi elucidates his solar nature:

"His policy of spiritual enlightenment was all-embracing. He inspired all alike and gave a lift to everyone in his religious, virtuous, moral, and spiritual life. He was never a leader of any one party. All parties found a common leader head in Him. All the various differences and dissensions of the various castes, creeds, and *sampradayas* dissolved in his Presence and every party felt to be a thread in the warp and woof of society, and that all the threads make the cloth, and that no thread can be taken out, with advantage, from it. Such was His Universality and all-embracing nature."

Additional Resources

Osho's book, *Krishna: the Man and his Philosophy*, is an excellent text on Surya Yoga and its paradoxical nature.

RAHU AND KETU
The North and South Nodes
of the Moon

The Nodes of the Moon-Rahu and Ketu-are not physical planets. They are called "shadow planets" because they hide the Sun and the Moon during eclipses.

In the ancient Vedic tradition, these two "planets" are sometimes treated as one and sometimes treated separately. They are shrouded in mystery. Even their physical form is shadowy in that they are not physical bodies but mathematical points in the heavens. These points exist where the Moon's ascending path (North Node, or Rahu) and descending path (South Node, or Ketu) in the sky each intersect the apparent path of the Sun on the celestial sphere (called the Sun's ecliptic).

Rahu is our desire, our rebelliousness, uniqueness, and diversity, that part of us that wants to shun authority and to rebel against the status quo, to break the boundaries of stagnation and conditioned existence and break out of the routine of life.

Ketu is our karma and spirituality. Ketu signifies the spiritual process of the refinement of materialization to spirit. It is considered a benefic spiritually and a malefic materially as it causes sorrow and loss which often turns a person away from the outer, material world and inward to the silent witness, the silent Presence within. Ketu is considered responsible for Self Realization. Ketu is an indicator of intelligence, wisdom, non-attachment, mysticism, penetrating insight, and psychic abilities.

Attributes

Just as the physical presence of Rahu and Ketu (the Nodes) is shadowy, so is their significance and meaning. They govern shadow activities, such as silent crime and behind-the- scenes plots against authority. Rahu relates to outer rebellion; Ketu to inner rebellion.

Rahu serves to purify society of outdated, rigid, or calcified conventions and institutions. Although he acts contrary to mainstream laws and ethics, he fills an essential role in evolution, just as sharks, vultures, and parasitic insects fill a huge need in biosystems. Honoring scavengers, rebels, and outcastes is essential for a balanced view of social systems.

A surface understanding of Rahu can be used to rationalize all kinds of criminal and psychopathic behavior. A deeper understanding empowers one to rebel against all forms of societal inculcation which block one from discovering one's own inner potential. Thus any rebelliousness which harms another rather than achieving higher ends is a perversion of this principle.

Life in society is busy and beset by innumerable and often contradictory do's and don'ts. The Rahu revels in silence and solitude, which may be seen as a form of rebellion against social obligations. But silence and occasional solitude are necessary for inner equilibrium.

Even outlawish and seemingly anti-social behavior can benefit society in unexpected ways. Knowingly or unknowingly, society's outcastes can contribute to the whole. Robin Hood is an excellent example of a North Nodian character who sought justice outside the law, robbing from the rich to give to the poor in order to redress inequality in the distribution of wealth and power.

Rahu represents the rebelliousness which brings a fundamental balance sometimes called "cosmic consciousness," where one's Self is experienced as separate from activity.

Ketu, the South Node of the Moon, gives the capacity to cut through the gross aspects of creation to the intense beauty and bliss of the subtler levels of creation in a state called God consciousness, and eventually to surrender this sublime beauty for the undifferentiated Absolute in Unity consciousness. These higher states require an even greater inner silence than cosmic consciousness, plus a more refined awareness of the external world. Ketu signifies God's grace and the opportunity to receive it.

Thus Ketu represents an even deeper revolution of the psyche than Rahu. In God consciousness one surrenders one's cosmic Self to the Divine, and thereby unlocks the subtle structure of creation to direct perception. Rahu strips away social conventions and restrictions; Ketu strips away deeper limitations on feeling and perception. The deepest knots in the heart are dissolved in tidal waves of love. One discovers that beauty is truly in the eye of the beholder, and that infinite beauty is everywhere.

Rahu and Ketu, respectively, represent the outer and inner aspects of personal transformation. Both Nodes cut through boundaries with quickness and ferocity. Rahu rebels against outer limitations, especially outmoded social conventions. Ketu strips away limiting belief structures, such as the belief that we need fame or fortune to be happy.

Rahu, the head of the dragon, represents outer rebellion and frees us from social constraints. Ketu, the tail of the dragon, represents inner surrender and frees us from egotistical attachments. At first glance, surrender may seem to contradict the rebel principle of the nodes. A deeper view sees that inner surrender is only possible when we cut ourselves free from the tyranny of social convention, egotistical attachments, and unconscious beliefs. Only when we are truly free can we surrender to the higher states of consciousness beyond cosmic consciousness.

All of the deeper knowledge of astrology is structured in consciousness; the knowledge of the Nodes is especially so. In other words, your knowledge of their energy and significance will depend on your level of consciousness.

The Nodes take on the energy and characteristics of the planets with which they are associated. This association is formed from planetary conjunction, aspect, or sign placement. However, the Nodes also have their own energy which is best described as rebellious, revolutionary, outlawish, iconoclastic, independent, different, unique, and special. If you study the spiritual path related to the Nodes (Tantra), you will understand how this energy works inwardly. If you study the characteristics of an outcaste or "untouchable", you will gain insight into the more outward nature of the Nodes.

Eastern and Western forms of astrology have not always agreed as to the differences between the North and South Nodes. In Eastern astrology, Rahu is akin to Saturn; Ketu is akin to Mars. They are both considered to be natural malefics. In Western astrology the North Node is considered to be akin to Jupiter and a natural benefic, whereas the South Node is akin to Saturn and a natural malefic. Confusions like this are bound to arise when dealing with these shadow planets. It is their nature to hide their workings in the world. For example, when the Nodes govern physical health, the diseases they bring cannot be diagnosed or treated through traditional means; only occult forms of treatment are effective.

I know one gentleman with the nodes in his field of Creative Play. One day his fiancée made the mistake of asking him to play tennis at her club in a conservative southern community. He had fun, but she and others at the club were taken aback. In fact, she almost ended the engagement. In other ways this gentleman is quite natural and even conservative, but in this one Field of Living – look out!

The ideal living place for the Nodes is a remote, forested region where they can hide like Robin Hood.

Gypsies are governed by the Nodes of the Moon.

Russia has a strong Nodian stamp to its character.

The North Node governs the southwest. Los Angeles is one of the most southwest points in the U.S., and many urban gangs stem from there.

Colombia sits at the most southwest portion of the northern hemisphere. This may explain why it is a center for international drug traffic.

The Nodes are the foot-soldiers who can often turn the tide of battle – by some unique heroic act which defies all logical analysis or convention.

Youth are most in touch with the energy of the Nodes, because they are the most idealistic and rebellious and they sense the spiritual nature of the times.

If we don't learn to use the Nodian energy in a spiritual way, we are in big trouble!

The Nodes are not inherently evil: they purify society of outmoded, outdated conventions and institutions. They help keep the four castes pure, modern, useful, and efficient. Without the Nodian energy, society would fall under its own weight of encrustation.

The Nodes pose a threat to society when not properly understood and expressed.

Nodian beings help us learn to distinguish what is valuable in custom and tradition from what isn't.

On the surface of life we may see a crass, materialistic, physically-based form of rebellion resulting in superficial changes in hairstyle, dress, and mode of conduct. At a deeper level we see a rebellion against regional and national identifications and interests in the religious, political, social, and racial spheres. This deeper rebellion is what can help us spiritually. The more superficial rebelliousness merely opens us up to the deeper possibility.

Symbol

no symbol – ephemeral, mysterious, no physical reality

Color

no color, colorless

Gemstone

The North Node is propitiated by wearing Hessonite Garnet; the South Node, by wearing Crysoberyl Cat's Eye.

Sound

No sound can put one in touch with the energy of the Nodes. Understanding why this is so is a good contemplative exercise.

Deity

Rakshasas

Light

Positive agent of change, alternative demonstrators of light, way showers of truth.

Shadow

Outlaw/criminal behavior, wanton destruction, egoic display of outlandishness.

Examples

Bhagwan Shree Rajneesh, later called Osho, was a great Tantric sage who formed a community of spiritual outlaws in Oregon. Naturally this community was seen as a great threat by the more conventional, largely conservative rural society around it, and was brought down by both internal weakness and external pressure.

Elvis Presley was a notable Nodian character. So was Mahatma Gandhi.

A controversial public figure often has the Nodes placed in the field of career, or some other prominent position in another Field of Living. Madonna is such a person.

Individuals who have great power, and whose career nature is governed by the Nodes, will use this power unlawfully. Richard Nixon was such a man. Interestingly, such a person finds it difficult to see what they did wrong – so natural and deeply rooted is this unlawful tendency.

The Path of the Iconoclast
the Rebel Path
Tantra

Finally we come to the rebel path of Tantra, the iconoclast, governed by the Nodes of the Moon which signify the rebel, the spiritual outlaw who follows the beat of her own drum, the iconoclast. Yoga focuses on effort and discipline, Tantra more on surrender and relaxation.

The term 'Tantra' is as vast and varied as 'yoga.' Tantra means "technique," and there are countless techniques in different tantric traditions. Tantra is flowing with desire without resisting, just accepting natural urges and becoming fully aware of every thought, every feeling, every moment. It is contrasted with yoga, which restrains and redirects desire. The yogi always keeps a firm hand on the floodgates of desire, permitting enough of a flow to maintain physical and emotional health, but never opening the gates wide. The Tantric throws the floodgates wide open, unafraid of the rushing torrent of desire.

For a true Tantrica, the mind transcends at the moment of desire fulfillment. Whereas many who are not true Tantricas run the danger of getting trapped in the never-ending cycle of desire fulfillment leading to more and more desires, the true Tantrica fulfills each desire with full attention, with conscious presence to each moment of the process of desire fulfillment.

Tantra is ruled by the "shadow" planets, the North and South Nodes of the Moon (Rahu and Ketu). The nodes are rebels, outlaws, and iconoclasts. They reject any authority except their own experience. They always reflect the energy of one of the other planets in a very unique and unconventional way, so Tantra is at least as vast and complex as all the yogas taken together.

Sensationalistic writers paint Tantra as the path to enlightenment through sex, alcohol, drugs, and black magic, while ignoring the devastation that can ensue from abandoning caution and concern for others. Any path can be corrupted! Tantra involves a sense of play and freedom from spiritual convention, but requires absolute adherence to one rule, Be conscious, remain fully aware at all times. So the hedonist who dulls his mind through overindulgence is as far from true Tantra as the celibate ascetic alone in his cave.

Real Tantra takes as much time and practice as yoga. Tantra, like yoga, requires full awareness in the present every moment of the day. Although "pop" tantra is generally associated with sexuality, most tantric techniques do not involve sex. The classic textbook of Tantra, the Vigyana Bhairava Tantra gives 112 different Tantric techniques, of which only three deal with sexuality. Many of them are simple awareness tools for enjoying nature or becoming aware of your mind, body, and emotions.

Unfortunately, without more guidance, most aspirants are befuddled by over-choice. If you are intimidated by the complexity of Tantra, you may need a master, or should be practicing yoga, not Tantra. The true Tantric delights in experimentation, and trusts his own experience far more than any guru.

Since Tantra plays directly with desire, it may be unsuitable for those whose inner nature is yogic (about seven people out of eight). Tantra is for the one of eight who are natural spiritual rebels, not just those who abhor outer authority and convention.

Please note that we are using the word "tantra" in a very different sense than Tibetan Buddhist Tantra. Lord Buddha was North nodian in his rejection of orthodox Hinduism and theism, but the term "Buddhist Tantra" is an oxymoron, as control of desire is central to all Buddhism. Tibetan Tantra is decidedly nontantric in its monastic discipline and veneration of authority.

Although India and Tibet are best known for Tantra, techniques of using desire to go beyond desire have existed in some form in every culture. There is another worldwide category of pseudo-religious practices that are related to the "left-handed path" of Tantra, but have nothing to do with genuine spiritual practices. These include black magic, Satanism, and esoteric power cults. The fact that all the paths have often been corrupted in no way detracts from the truth of their pure forms.

In astrological terms, the strength of the ruling planet governs the purity of its path for any given individual. Someone with a strong Moon governing his spirituality will lead a very compassionate life, while the same path ruled by a weak or afflicted Moon may be cruel or obsessed by psychic power trips. The way to remedy the planetary affliction and advance spiritually is always to steer toward the positive qualities of the planet involved, such as unselfish love, harmony, or truth.

Mastery of desire is central to all forms of yoga, although most practices sublimate desire rather than confronting it directly. In the Bhagavad Gita Lord Krishna, the Lord of Yogis, tells Arjuna that it is desire, "all-consuming and most evil," which impels man to commit sin, even involuntarily, as if driven by force. "Know this to be the enemy here on earth."

The secret to success in Tantra is understanding desire as a friend, not an enemy. Desire is a friend we cannot live without. The only people who succeed in Tantra are those who can appreciate the deeper levels of desire without getting lost in surface desire. Our deepest desire is for enlightenment- absolute freedom, bliss, and love. The danger is that surface desires often flow in the opposite direction of spiritual desires.

The Tantric cultivates awareness of the flow of desire and, like the yogi, avoids attachment to the objects of desire. Desire for objects takes you out of the present. Awareness of the flow of desire keeps you in the present. Gradually, awareness of the flow grows into awareness of the silent source of desire. Then you become master of desire, not its slave.

To feel that you NEED something in order to be happy is to surrender your bliss and power to something outside of you, whether you are a yogi or a tantric.

The most articulate and enlightened modern tantric was Osho, previously known as Bhagavan Shree Rajneesh. He was a brilliant psychologist and outspoken critic of all that suppresses the human spirit, to the point that he encouraged his followers not to believe him, but to make up their own minds and not accept his authority on anything. He was surrounded by scandal, vilified by the press, and allegedly poisoned by U.S. Government officials prior to his expulsion from the U.S. for immigration fraud. His followers included both criminals and saints. A Tantric to the core, he invited controversy and seemed to love being hated. Blasting orthodoxy and reveling in controversy is typical Rahu behavior, and no one surpassed Osho in this respect!

The Nodes of the Moon move in a left-handed direction (Aries to Pisces), whereas all the other planets move in a right-handed direction (Pisces to Aries). Thus astronomy itself gives a visible demonstration and confirmation of the left- (Tantra) and right-handed paths (Yoga) to Self Realization.

The practical handbook of Tantra is *The Vigyana Bhairava Tantra*. Some call it the spiritual encyclopedia of life because it delineates all of the different possible methods of meditation. Lore has it that it was written by Lord Shiva, which means it was 'divinely inspired.' Osho's *Book of Secrets* is a commentary on the underlying basis for these techniques and why there can be only 112 of them. Osho states that some individuals might think there are too many techniques to try to understand, much less experiment with. However, this handbook, in its entirety, is meant primarily for Tantric individuals and serves three purposes:

- It strips away the spiritual authority of those whose power is based on fraudulent claims of exclusive techniques;
- It requires a highly developed Tantric for research and experimentation in spiritual matters;
- It allows a Tantric to skillfully use earthly desires and passions as a path to enlightenment.

There are 7 paths to Self Realization (Yogas) – through body, senses, heart, mind, intellect, subtle body, and through all of them. Nyaya Philosophy states that to be fully grasped, any subject must be approached from 16 angles. 16 angles of approach times 7 paths equals 112 techniques.

The Vigyana Bhairava Tantra can also be used by Yoga practitioners; however, they must focus in an integral way on the 16 techniques related to their path, rather than all the techniques.

A Tantric sage often loves to argue and shock. When Osho formed a community of rebels around him in Oregon, sparks were bound to fly. A good rebel sage always creates 'trouble' wherever she/he goes. Most Yogic teachers conduct their lecture in an atmosphere of sanctity. Only a Tantric teacher like Osho would dare give an uproariously funny lecture on the various uses of the word "fuck"!

The things often denounced by Yoga practitioners (sex, wine, meat, drugs, etc.) are greatly valued by Tantrics as tools of their trade. The same holds true for conventionally 'disgusting' things like meditating on corpses in Indian burial grounds, or group sex, or many other forms of seemingly aberrant or anti-social behavior.

A Tantric sage will often be the enemy of the more conventionally minded in society.

Many Tantricas prefer to do their practices in secret to avoid being harassed by society at large. However, a true teacher of Tantra has no such luxury if she/he hopes to influence large segments of society.

Many potential Tantricas are suppressed so thoroughly by society that they aren't even aware of it. This can be particularly true of female disciples in organizations having a yogic orientation.

Tantricas will tend to experiment with one of the 112 techniques for a period of at least three months, then move on to another technique. This process continues until they find THE technique.

To say that one is a disciple of a Tantric master is a contradiction in terms. Tantricas need primarily to be their own teachers, while at the same time remaining open to any valuable knowledge provided by the Tantric master. In fact, this is how to identify a true Tantric teacher; he will totally respect your independence in a novel way.

It can be uncomfortable to find your way in the darkness. But a mature Tantric wouldn't have it any other way.

Additional Resources

Osho's *Book of Secrets*

Autobiography of a Spiritually Incorrect Mystic by Osho

Desire

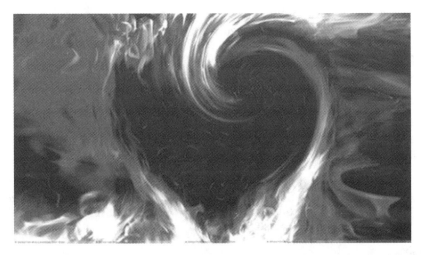

We have innumerable desires every day. Consciously or subconsciously, each desire confronts us with a primordial decision-what to do with it? We want to sleep, but have to work. We want to shop, but need to save. We want to be with someone, but that someone does not want to be with us. We want to rid the world of war, crime, disease, corruption, and pollution, but feel that we do not have the power. We want to live forever, but .... ad infinitum!

There are four possible responses to any desire:

1. Redirect its energy into something safer or more constructive

2. Satisfy it while recognizing that is small and fleeting

3. Suppress or deny it

4. Indulge it blindly without awareness

These four choices correspond to the four basic approaches to spirituality:

1. Yoga – restraint or moderation of desire, redirection/sublimation of destructive energies.

2. Tantra – Flowing with desire without getting drowned.

3. Surface control – trying to change outer behavior without refining inner awareness-the approach of conventional ethics, whether religious or not.

4. Hedonism and any form of blind self-gratification without concern for others or long-term consequences.

We can illustrate these primordial options with a diagram:

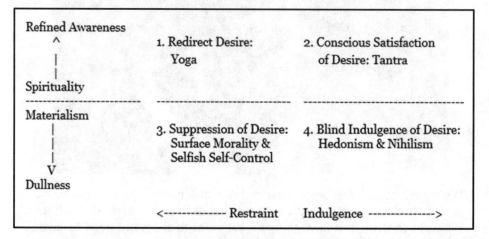

On the vertical axis we find whatever means the most to us, spiritual values or material ones. Higher is the direction of increasing awareness, harmony, love, and bliss; lower is the direction of increasing dullness, tension, separateness, and misery. On the horizontal axis is our approach, restraint or indulgence of desire.

Hedonism and nihilism are a vicious circle. Satiating the senses leaves one feeling empty and wasted (nihilism) . This creates cravings to fill the void with more indulgence. And so the addiction cycle continues. Hollywood and Madison Avenue thrive on feeding this addiction. So if you are serious about spirituality in any form, cut back on the mass media and put your attention on more elevating recreations, such as meditation, spiritual gatherings, and communion with nature.

The reason the world is in a fix is that most people live in the bottom half of the diagram, in deep denial of their spiritual essence. Suppression of desire is a hot topic in modern psychology, but suppression of spiritual experience is far more damaging to the individual and society. Organized religions, at least in the West, have inadvertently collaborated in the growth of materialism by fostering blind faith, dogma, and dependence on external authority (the religious institution or leader). Spirituality and creativity can only blossom in an environment of freedom and respect for differences of experience and opinion.

The danger of Tantra is that few people can really flow with desire without being drowned.

Natural-born yogis, who are happiest in the first quadrant, get sucked into the fourth quadrant whirlpool if they try to practice Tantra. We all have to follow some desires, but as a spiritual path, Tantra is for the few, not the many. Excessive sensory indulgence is poison for most spiritual aspirants.

It is a great mistake to think that one can take the best of Yoga and Tantra as a spiritual practice, alternating periods of great restraint with periods of wanton excess. Just as it is hard on the physical body to alternate between fasting and gorging, it is hard on the spiritual body to alternate between restraint and indulgence of desire. After experiencing both ascetism and luxury, Lord Buddha taught the middle path, a balance between restraint and indulgence that can be maintained for a lifetime.

It is no wonder Tantrics have been so despised by those who struggle to master desire! The human population is roughly equally distributed among the eight paths. About one-eighth are meant to practice each of these archetypal paths. Unfortunately, most are not really practicing any spiritual path beyond the first level, surface morality.

Conclusion:
Determining Your Spiritual Nature

Although many or most of us have at one time or another experienced the transcendence of the mind, or an experience of unity or oneness with all creation, through many or even all of these paths, Edward hypothesized that there is one path that is the primary path for each individual.

It is important to realize that no one path is right for everyone, for every mind, though most spiritual teachers are strong advocates of a particular path, as it is the one that "worked" for them.

Which planet predominates in our Spiritual Nature determines the way we will most effectively transcend the mind and realize pure awareness as our essential nature. However, all of the planetary energies are alive within all of us, each predominantly influencing a different area of our lives. Which planet predominates in our Spiritual Nature and which predominate in each area of our life are given by our Spiritual Blueprint™.

Determining our spiritual blueprint is not an exact science. At the time of Edward's transition, he felt he had found the exact determination of an individual's spiritual nature, as well as what planet primarily governs each area of an individual's life, the Fields of Living. However, he always regarded this determination as hypothetical, as informed guidance to be tested with our personal experience.

Since Edward's ascension, Bernadette Cardinale, Edward's beloved partner and Spiritual Science and Consciousness researcher, has received additional insight regarding the proper method of determining one's spiritual nature, and one's entire Spiritual Blueprint™ which includes all of the Fields of Living, which many people feel is even more accurate.

You may receive an individual Spiritual Blueprint™ reading from either Bernadette or Orion. In this reading you will be given your unique Spiritual Nature, as well as where each of the planets reside in each of your Fields of Living, revealing to you the primary influence, or perspective, you have in that field.

doorwaystoawakening.com/spiritual-blueprints

However, in addition to your being given this individualized reading, we encourage you to read the different spiritual paths and see for yourself which one, or ones, resonate most for you. Be ruthlessly honest with yourself. Which of these approaches gives you the best results?

"The subjective spiritual blueprint should be treated as a scientific hypothesis rather than as established fact, and it is certainly offered in that spirit." ~ Edward Tarabilda

Chapter 8
The Fields of Living

In addition to your Spiritual Nature, there are seven additional Fields of Living, areas of life. These are your:

- Dharma or Caste nature
- Primal Desire nature
- Relating style
- Career nature
- Creative Play nature
- Mental nature
- Physical nature

As we have now become somewhat familiar with each of the planetary energies and have seen how each indicates and influences our spiritual nature, we will now see how they influence all of the other areas of our life. When a particular planet is the predominant energy influencing a particular field of life, we will feel and experience that influence, and see how it affects the way we perceive and act within that field.

Once again, we must consider the issue of free will versus determinism. How much of our actions are determined by these planetary influences and their governance of each Field of Living? The answer lies in each person's personal experience of that field, but also in the awareness of these influences and how they create almost like a force field, a predominant energy field within each of these areas of our lives. We will then find that when we go with the flow of that energy, instead of paddling upstream against it, life will be easier and more enjoyable and supported in success and fulfillment. In other words, we will feel like we are flowing with the current of life, like paddling downstream. Although the river of life that we are paddling on may have a definite direction and energetic tendency, we may find we can still steer within that stream and fill in the details by the choices we make. The journey can either be one of ease and going with the flow, or one of struggle and hardship because we have some concept of how we should be or what our life should look like which is counter to the reality of what is.

In other words, when we investigate and understand and accept that these are the planetary influences within each field, we will learn how to navigate the waters of life skillfully and enjoyably.

Dharma
The Field of Caste Nature

Dharma is action to uphold society, how to serve others in a way that brings maximum fulfillment to all. The great civilizations of antiquity had three or four major divisions of labor. These divisions were perhaps clearest in the four castes of ancient India:

- Brahmins - priests, counselors, and teachers, serving society through higher knowledge and religion
- Kshatriyas - rulers, administrators, warriors, and doctors, serving by protecting the physical welfare of society
- Vaishyas - merchants and farmers, serving through trade and finance
- Shudras - craftsmen and manual laborers, serving through crafts and physical labor
- Outcastes - those whose service to society is to root out impurities.

The field of Dharma is sometimes also called 'Caste Nature', but we tried to avoid this term as it is fraught with so many misconceptions and judgments and reinforces an artificial notion of the class system which has contributed to the oppression of people in India for centuries.

The hereditary caste system that prevails in India today is a cultural abomination. For perhaps four or five thousand years caste has been based on parentage, not the natural inclinations of each individual. When people are barred from practicing a preferred profession they suffer enormous job stress, and the creativity and productivity of the whole nation suffers. The higher castes use the system as an excuse to exploit the lower castes, so that caste becomes a means of undermining society, rather than strengthening it. The hereditary caste system is the clearest indication that India lost the inner keys to astrology at least three to five thousand years ago, since the whole idea of hereditary caste contradicts the principle of determining caste from one's birth chart and personal inclinations.

The Vedic caste system was originally based on each individual's natural inclinations, not heredity. No one should be forced to follow a given caste or barred from a given caste against his or her will.

And, the word "dharma" has been defined in so many ways as to almost lose all specific meaning. Here we mean the Field of Living that relates to moral, ethical, and evolutionary behavior. How do we determine that action which is moral and ethical? According to the ancient sages, that action is moral and ethical which is motivated by selfless service to society. How do we best give to society? By knowing our caste nature and joyously performing it each day in a selfless manner.

The whole idea of dharma, as revealed through the Art of Multidimensional Living™, is that we have different ways of serving with joy and love. People who receive Spiritual Blueprint consultations invariably find this conception of caste and dharma confirms their natural inclinations in how to serve society.

The planets that are significators of each of these 'castes' are:

Jupiter, Venus	Brahmin
Mars, Sun	Kshatriya
Mercury, Moon	Vaishya
Saturn	Shudra
Nodes of the Moon, Rahu/Ketu	Outcaste

Brahmins are the priests, counselors, educators of society. They lead the cultural/religious/ educational caste institution, giving knowledge to society, especially spiritual knowledge.

Kshatriyas are the warriors in society, protecting society physically and sometimes spiritually (protecting through knowledge). Whereas Brahmins lead society in the pursuit of higher knowledge, Kshatriyas lead society in an external way, protecting society physically. They head the legal/political arm of society. Government officials, individuals in the military, policemen, firemen, doctors, lawyers – all these people are members of the warrior caste.

130

Vaishyas are the business class. They lead in the economic arena by providing the material resources which allow society to prosper.

Shudras serve one of the above mentioned castes, but not in a servile way unless the Shudra nature is weak. Shudras are very independent people who must learn to serve in a way that does not interfere with their love of freedom and privacy.

Outcastes are the rebels who purify society of its outmoded, outdated conventions. They prefer to live on the fringes of society. Gypsies are a good example of outcastes. Outcastes serve the other castes only when they have to, and even then, very independently.

Brahmins are not more interested in knowledge than members of other castes. However, they use it more effectively and creatively to bring spiritual help to society. They have more originality in the organization and use of higher knowledge.

Regardless of one's caste nature, a person can wake up to the truth of who they are as pure awareness.

One of the greatest thinkers of our age was a Kshatriya named S. Radhakrishnan, whose motivation and skills were directed more toward the compilation, protection, and preservation of Indian philosophy than toward making original contributions. Many of his admirers and critics have recognized and commented on this very fact.

In the ancient days, Vaishyas were most often farmers who used their land to support the other castes. Only later did they begin to be primarily merchants and manufacturers.

Outcastes are a greater threat to society when we resist their nature or their potential contribution to society. The homeless are sometimes outcastes who voluntarily choose this lifestyle over conventional living. Homeless people who are not outcastes are usually forced by economic or other circumstance into this adverse situation.

Rasputin was an outcaste. He spent much of his life traveling in gypsy-like fashion throughout Russia until he finally found favor with the royal family. His scandalous lifestyle and behavior while with them contributed to the fall of this family from power. Their failure to heed his often sage advice and to place curbs on his rebellious nature were two giant mistakes which wiser rulers would never have made.

Caste is the most important factor in determining marriage compatibility, but astrologers no longer know how to judge caste (or any other important criteria) in any of the eight Fields of Living. Thus, their so-called compatibility studies are misleading.

The ancient sages understood why you should only marry within your own caste. This no longer makes sense to us. Individuals who have different caste natures expend their energies in different directions; when functioning together, their wholeness is less than the sum of the parts. Those having the same caste nature create a wholeness greater than the sum of its parts.

Most people find the way to their true caste nature on their own, but it may take them almost a lifetime to do so, and some never find it. Without the necessary validation, even those who find it may not fully appreciate it.

When you ask yourself, "How can I best serve society?", you are asking a dharmic question.

Moral and ethical questions often have an emotional component. This is why one spouse will say to another, "That's not fair!" when having some disagreement. In this sense, caste incompatibility undermines emotional compatibility.

The *Bhagavad Gita* says, "Better one's own dharma, no matter how lowly, than the dharma of another. "It is impossible to be totally content when one is out of dharma.

One can speak of "spiritual dharma," (Edward) but I prefer to use the word exclusively in describing one's moral and ethical obligation. At least one should distinguish spiritual and moral dharma.

Paul Brunton, from his *Notebooks*: "Dharma = moral living."

At the surface of life lie the three great social values: liberty, fraternity, and equality. At the subtle levels of existence lie *sattwa*, *rajas*, and *tamas*. At the core of existence lie *sat*, *chit*, and *ananda*. The ability to grasp with certitude all these various interrelationships is important, especially for those on the path of Gyana Yoga.

A great debate exists between two castes. Brahmins have traditionally been in charge of creating, maintaining, and revising spiritual knowledge, and yet, there is also an ancient tradition which gives Kshatriyas responsibility for maintaining its purity and efficacy. Are there both mundane and cosmological reasons for this latter tradition?

A weak caste nature makes individuals confused and indecisive about moral and ethical questions; they can be thrown into an ethical quandary quite easily. This will, in turn, wreak havoc on their emotions.

A person with a weak caste nature needs a moral advisor!

A weak caste nature is a possessive one. Attachment to a particular moral position or perspective creates more problems than it solves.

134

Primal Desire
The Field of Wealth

The Field of Wealth governs the strength and nature of our deepest desires. Although it is by no means limited to material desires, it affects our prosperity by shaping our confidence and motivation for material wealth.

Here are the Primal desires:

Sun: Desire for leadership and sometimes adulation
Moon: Desire for deep emotional bonding
Mars: Desire for self-sufficiency and power
Mercury: Desire for all forms of deep, esoteric knowledge and the opportunity to express it
Jupiter: Desire for community and fellowship with others.
Venus: Desire for ideal love relationships and beauty in all its forms
Saturn: Desire for a more private, simple life
Nodes of the Moon: Desire to be a rebel, revolutionary, outlaw and to purify society of outdated, outmoded conventions and institutions

Wealth is more than our objective resources such as money, land, conveyances, good reputation, etc. It is also the ability to fulfill our most primal desires. A man may have lots of money and property, yet still be frustrated over his inability to achieve some primal need.

Some people know exactly what they want in life. Others spend a life-time trying to figure out what they want. The first type has clear desires; the second type suffers from a lack of direction. The planet ruling wealth governs the strength and nature of our deepest desires.

Saturn, for example, is the simplest and most reclusive planet. If he governs your wealth nature, you value privacy and simplicity, longevity, and a good physique. However, if Jupiter rules your wealth, then you value family, proper conduct, and a more opulent lifestyle. If the Sun rules your wealth, then you love to shine in public, and you may dream of being a famous celebrity or politician.

This Field of Living defines what we seek for temporal fulfillment and happiness. It defines the nature of our primal desires. Once again, each of the planets delineates one of the eight primal desires.

Once you understand more about the planets and their significations, you can expand the brief descriptions given above.

The desire nature should not be suppressed in any way because it leads us to our own unique form of temporal happiness and fulfillment. However, neither should it be trusted in that it often seeks to usurp the planet governing the spiritual life by confusing temporal fulfillment with the lasting fulfillment of enlightenment. This enlightenment can only come through following the guidance of the planet governing our spiritual nature.

For example, if someone has Saturn governing their desire nature and the Sun governing their spiritual nature, then, at some period in their life, they may wrongly assume that by following a more reclusive, disciplined, private sort of existence, they will be more likely to gain enlightenment. In reality they need to use a more liberal, expanded, solar approach.

Thus, the desire nature can be a great seducer, which always promises much more than it delivers, especially in relation to the spiritual life.

Obviously, desires do not always lead to fulfillment. How fully we achieve our desires depends on all eight fields of living. A weakness in any field may sap energy from other fields. It is also possible for two fields to be in conflict. For example, an individual who has a soft Venusian spiritual nature and an aggressive Mars desire nature frequently feels pulled between peace and war. Whenever such conflicts arise our advice is to let the spiritual nature lead, as it is the unifying factor in the personality.

Let us give a couple of examples regarding prosperity. A weak Mars governing wealth means a person tends to lose money through lack of energy to follow through. A weak Moon means a person swings in great waves of emotion from one desire to another, lacking the steadiness to achieve anything significant.

Understanding our desires is a wonderful aid for mastering them. The distinction between our spiritual nature and desire nature is particularly valuable. It helps us resolve inner conflict and recognize our sattwic (positive) attachments. For example, a Jupiterian desire nature may make us judgmental- we may pay more attention to others' morality than our own. If spirituality is our priority, it is easy to turn our attention to something naturally fulfilling in accord with our spiritual path.

In the Far East there is an adage: "Treat your desire nature as you would a cobra. Give the cobra milk, make it happy, but don't trust it." We should use this same approach with our desire nature. Don't suppress it, keep it happy, but don't trust it.

Any time there is a conflict between your innermost spiritual nature and your desire nature, go with your inner nature. It will never disappoint you.

If we suppress our desire nature, it expresses itself in the most inappropriate ways. The psychologists and psychiatrists are right when they warn of the dangers of emotional suppression.

If a person has Venus governing his/her desire nature and some other planet governing his/her spiritual nature, he/she will from time to time fall under the illusion that he/she needs an ideal love relationship to be successful spiritually. They will also likely fall under some attachment to Raja Yoga, the path of beauty and art. In time, they will learn not to trust this desire nature in relation to spiritual questions.

This Field of Living defines one's *sattwic* attachments – attachments which are so primal and which seem so right, just, good, pure, noble, etc., that one has trouble even recognizing the attitude or behavior as an attachment, much less being able to rid oneself of it.

Knowing one's primal desire nature helps individuals know their blind spot in relationship to spiritual life. So many people waste so much time chasing their desire nature in the hope that it will bring permanent and lasting peace and bliss. Alas, it will only bring fleeting happiness, fleeting satisfaction! It is meant to be subordinate to the spiritual quest.

Sattwic attachment to the guru is particularly hard to overcome for those whose desire nature is governed by the Moon or Jupiter.

Those who have a Mercurial desire nature hunger after knowledge, but seldom gain lasting fulfillment from it. Eventually, they may even throw away their books in disgust.

Those whose desire nature is ruled by Mars can be fooled into believing that their interest in Tantra, and its sexual techniques, is purely spiritual.

If one's desire nature is ruled by the Sun, then the person favors a very liberal approach to spirituality, including an early emphasis on short-path techniques. This is the illusion they must overcome to make headway in the spiritual life.

I know a gentleman who has a Mercurial spiritual nature and a Nodian desire nature. He has never had his predominant strength of personality identified, and thus, has not learned how to use this strength (the intellect) as a specific, spiritual tool. Consequently, he is seduced into believing that a rebellious approach to everything spiritual serves him best. To those around him it is apparent that this approach does not serve him well and merely makes him cynical.

Someone with a Saturnine desire nature and a Solar spiritual nature will face a major conflict in his life: how, when, and where to be inward and private, so as not to wrongly usurp the solar requirement of public leadership and responsibility.

When the planet governing this Field of Living is weak overall, the person often feels that he has no important worldly goal to strive for; he feels listless and adrift. This can be doubly painful if he has no strong spiritual life or aspirations.

If the planet governing this Field of Living is debilitated, the person will be very attached to fulfilling his primal desires. This pursuit will leave him frustrated, since no permanent fulfillment can ever come from this pursuit. He is most likely to remain mired in illusion.

While being suspicious of our primal desires, it is important not to suppress them in any way. The desire nature is a powerful horse which we should ride freely, but which we should also consciously control; otherwise, we will be thrown off and become injured. So by all means, ride the horse of desire with great vigor and joyfulness, but be alert during the ride. Make sure you are guiding the horse and not vice versa!

The Field of Wealth also governs how well we hold onto the money that we acquire through our career nature, play nature, inheritances, etc.

138

What we value as wealth has a great influence over the kind of wealth we acquire, and how much.

The self-justifications, which take place through the desire nature, are humorous when looked at from a higher perspective.

Saturn: When the desire nature is ruled by Saturn, the person feels that by "playing it safe" religiously and spiritually, he has the best chance of Self Realization. This will most likely be an illusion and can keep him from fully using his more inward spiritual nature if he is not careful.

Venus: If, however, Venus governs the desire nature, then there is considerable danger of delusion in the quest for an ideal lover and companion. The ideal mate will always promise more than s/he delivers, as far as the spiritual life is concerned.

Mars: Those with a desire nature ruled by Mars first seek power over themselves (self-sufficiency), then power over others. They desire to take active steps to influence or change others in some way.

Moon: Those who have the Moon ruling their desire nature often suffer the illusion that an intimate love relationship is necessary to their spiritual evolution or underlying happiness.

Mercury: When Mercury governs the desire nature, the person becomes fascinated with knowledge – and later, disappointed with it.

Jupiter: When Jupiter governs the desire nature, then the path of selfless service and its counterpart (the path of religion) have the potential to fool or delude us by promising more than they deliver.

Sun: A solar desire nature tends to make one a spiritual dabbler. If one's desire nature is ruled by the Sun, then one will tend to prematurely take to the Short Path for Self Realization. One will emphasize one's kingship before having been a crown prince!

Rahu/Ketu: When the Nodes govern the field of wealth or primal desires, the person is deluded into thinking that Tantra will be his salvation, especially its sexual aspects.

Relating Style
The Field of Relationships

The Field of Relationships is the way we relate to other people. This field of living includes interpersonal interactions with parents, siblings, children, relatives, friends, and associates.

There are eight basic styles of relating and each person naturally favors one of these styles over the other seven. Which style a person favors can be determined by knowing which planet governs this field of living.

Sun: Charismatic, liberal, confident, and authoritative
Moon: Empathetic, caring, loving, and nourishing
Mars: Bold, assertive, direct, willful, and straight to the point
Mercury: Flexible, adaptable, fun-loving, and good with words
Jupiter: Giving, serving, and balanced in approach
Venus: Sweet, romantic, compromising, and idealistic
Saturn: Self-sufficient, private, reclusive, reliable, sincere, dutiful
Nodes: Rebellious and iconoclastic

We have myriad relationships in family, school, work, and play. Throughout all of these, one planetary archetype governs our prevailing style. When the ruling planet is strong, we tend to relate well, and vice versa if the ruling planet is weak.

One special relationship for most people is the lover or spouse. The same planet that governs relationships in general also governs sexuality and intimacy. However, intimacy is only one aspect of marriage.

Marriage is actually governed by the interaction of all eight fields, especially dharma, spirituality, creative play, and relating style. Compatibility assessment is available as an add-on to one's Spiritual Blueprint consultation which can prevent decades of frustration and wasted effort in incompatible relationships. If two partners have severe incompatibilities, no amount of counseling will fix the problem. Compatibility consultations can identify the strengths and weaknesses of a relationship, and suggest ways to avoid conflict and enhance the harmony. They are relevant and valuable to all types of relationships, including business partnerships and parent-child interactions.

For example, if a strong Moon rules your relationships, you have deep compassion and sensitivity for the needs of others. People seek your company for the nourishment they feel in your presence. On the other hand, if a strong Sun rules your relationships, you have a confident, generous, extroverted style with others. A friend with a strong Sun is a born politician and spontaneous entertainer. When he walks into a party, his charisma lights up the room. If instead of an exalted Sun, his relating style were ruled by a debilitated or malefic Sun, he might come across as a domineering tyrant.

Edward consulted with an individual whose relating style is governed by a debilitated Jupiter. He finds no joy relating to others, especially if the interactions are long or intense. He is like a shallow well. After a few words he dries up with nothing left to give.

A weakness in any field of life can often be overcome by strengths in other fields. For example, if one's relating style is weak, but career nature or mental health quotient is strong, it will ameliorate the lack of relating skills.

When we understand the different relating styles, we become more sensitive and tolerant. A Saturn relating style is often mistaken for aloofness or lack of concern. Saturn, of course, is by nature secretive and reclusive. S/he is silent and self-sufficient. Although independent, they are pillars of strength in times of crisis. A friend has an exalted Saturn governing this field. He voluntarily lives thousands of miles from his wife and children. He loves them dearly, but a few months of family life every year or two provide enough intimacy for him. Conventional thinking would say he has a problem that needs fixing. We say he is following his natural instinct correctly, and is evidently happy with his family life. His wife and children may not be happy with his choices, but that's a compatibility issue requiring a deeper look at their lives, too. If they have similar Saturnine relating styles, they probably value all the privacy they can get.

142

Our ability to be sexual and intimate with one special partner is also determined from this field of living.

One style of relating is not better than any other, but in our minds we often try to make it so.

Early family life is a training ground for how skillfully we relate with others later in life.

Courses on finding the right mate, or keeping one's mate, are very popular these days. However, they tend to overemphasize how to get our spouse or lover to satisfy our needs; they subtly reinforce the ego structure.

Those who insist on criticizing us in some way are, most often, the very people we should listen to least. It is usually some projection on their part.

If you are troubled by some behavior of another, realize that the source of the discomfort lies in you. Use it as an opportunity for introspection.

If we never give our close friends permission to critique us in any way, this is a sign that we are protecting our fragile ego structures.

If someone insists on giving you some criticism, and it is apparent that they are projecting some inner discomfort onto you, there is no need to respond in any way. Let them have their say and keep silent. Or, at the end of their tirade, say: "It sounds like you have a problem, which you need to address." This forces them to look at their own issues rather than encouraging further projection towards you. Of course, they may not like you for it.

No rule is absolute. Sometimes a good friend must criticize another close friend, without being asked to do so, in order to attempt to keep the friendship. The same holds true for other types of relationships: lovers, parents and children, business partners, etc.

Heart-oriented individuals will often use a different approach than rejecting unsolicited criticism or advice. They will say to the person: "Yes, please tell me how I might act in a better, more skillful way. Please help me." This approach tends to be more popular and disarming, because the other person does not have to look and see whether or not they are projecting rather than stating objective fact.

If you must criticize, be balanced in your approach. Focus on the positive as well as the negative; speak gently and compassionately.

143

When the planet governing this field of living is weak, the person is very attached to good relationships, sexuality, and intimacy. This attachment breeds many problems and evils.

When you reach a certain level of spiritual development, you will realize that there is only one key to effective relationships: don't ask others to be different from who they are, and don't allow others to require you to be different either. It sounds simple, but how difficult this is for us in practice!

The ego wants everyone else to think, feel, and act the same as it does. However, this would bring boredom to life.

It is easy to argue back and forth about who is being egotistical. How can we really tell? Those individuals are "in their ego" who demand something of someone else because of some inner discomfort. This is a good rule of thumb.

This mode of communication will be difficult at first, but try to say things like: "I feel that you are never there when I need you," rather than: "You are never there when I need you." The second statement states something as an objective fact and raises resistance.

Arguments are rarely over factual issues; they involve issues of fairness and ethics. This is why the caste nature of both individuals should be the same: they will have a similar perspective on moral and ethical issues and will also share an emotional affinity with respect to them.

Emotions and ethics go hand in hand.

I teach the friendship model for marriage and intimate relationships. Treat your intimate partner no different than you would treat your best friends. Negotiated commitments don't work well with friends – why do we assume they will work well with a lover?

Wake up each morning wanting for your lover exactly what he or she would want, even if this means his or her temporary or permanent departure.

Come together when it is a joy, otherwise remain independent.

Don't use children as an excuse for violating or negating the friendship model. Only have children if you, and you alone, are willing to raise them. This is not to suggest that both parents do not have a moral duty to raise their children properly; only that one spouse does not have the right to tell the other spouse when and how to carry out that duty.

I don't need someone to tell me that she will stay with me until she dies. Such a requirement comes from the ego's need for security.

Relationship is not based in obligation; it is a heart connection.

Marriage is part of the field of living known as physicality, not the field of relationships. Only sexuality and intimacy are part of the field of relationships. This is why some individuals may have a wonderful relationship while they court each other, but a poor one once they start sharing physical space.

The relationship among siblings is a great testing ground for developing relationship skills.

The practice of obtaining a compatibility study before one marries is out of vogue in our culture. This omission was wise when a true, spiritual science of the stars did not exist. Now it does exist.

Strong compatibility in the field of spiritual life definitely helps offset caste incompatibility in the field of dharma.

Caste compatibility does not ensure a good marriage, especially if the spiritual natures are incompatible, or divergent in maturation.

In some cases a field of living other than dharma or spiritual life may be the glue of a particular relationship: shared career, shared play nature, etc.

One can have strong outward compatibility and weak inward compatibility, or vice versa. Inward compatibility is more qualitative, which means individuals may share the same likes and dislikes. Outward compatibility relates more to outward timing, place, and circumstance. For example, two individuals may love to play tennis, but find it difficult to agree on the time and place. Of the two forms of compatibility, the inward is more important. Nevertheless, it is best to have both forms in as many fields of living as possible.

Saturn: When Saturn governs interpersonal relationships, it brings a style which is best described as private, reclusive, self-sufficient and yet dutiful and reliable especially in a crisis situation..

Venus: When Venus governs interpersonal relationships, it makes one an expert in romance and courtship; one is a real "smoothie"!

Mars: In the field of relationships Mars can be quite assertive and direct. When Mars is malefic or weak, it can bring an "in-your-face" style of relating which others find disconcerting.

When Mars governs the field of interpersonal relationships, the individual is cognizant of the polarity with the opposite sex and enjoys active, adventurous activities.

Moon: The Moon's relating style is compassionate, empathetic, and nourishing, like a mother with her children.

Mercury: Mercury brings deep, clear, and insightful communication to the field of interpersonal relationships. However, Mercury only has limited energy (neuter planet) for this activity.

Jupiter: If the field of interpersonal relationships is governed by Jupiter, then the person tends to enjoy social interaction. This is one reason he tends to do it well; the other is his sense of selfless service while interacting.

Sun: The Sun relating style thrives in spiritual community or high governmental organizations, especially as its leader. However, the Sun is often considered arrogant, proudful by less Self Actualized individuals.

Rahu/Ketu: The Nodes of the Moon style will eschew conventional interpersonal relationships. They will chart their own, original, iconoclastic relationship course to the beat of their own drum. They are masters of deception.

Career Nature
The Field of Career

What career are you best suited for?

Everyone has all eight planetary energies, each one ruling a different field of living. One of these governs how we best express ourselves in work. Dharma, creativity, and motivation all play a role in career success. But the most important factor is the intelligence available in our pursuit of a career. The field of career governs work, how we best exert ourselves day after day, year after year, in the pursuit of a livelihood. Our daily activity also serves to support spiritual progress by integrating and stabilizing pure awareness.

This field is intimate for life mission as well. One's dharma will give further clarifications of one's career nature. Let us take a practical example: If one's caste nature is ruled by the Sun (which makes one a member of the Warrior caste) and one's career nature is ruled by Mars, one is more likely to be a policeman, fireman, surgeon, military leader, etc. If the caste nature is ruled by Mercury or the Moon, making one a member of the Business caste, then Mars in the career nature will make one a business supervisor or leader. Thus, career counseling which does not take into consideration a person's caste nature will be faulty, or at least inadequate.

It is invaluable to know the ruling archetype of this field in order to choose a career we can succeed in.

Each planet governs a different type of career. These are general categories and it is up to each individual to find his way to the specific career that is a reflection of both his dharma and career nature.

Each planetary career-type is roughly defined by the royal position held by that planet in the planetary cabinet or family. Here is a summary:

Sun = King: Multi-faceted career, leadership, entrepreneurship. Or any position related to the science of community-building and management. The Sun also indicates a career as a doctor.

Moon = Queen: Positions of nourishment such as a nurse, food distributor, dairy farmer, day-care mother, den-mother, etc. Or any position related to the exposition and use of myth and archetype.

Mars = Commander-In-Chief: Protective, supervisory roles such as soldier, fireman, trial lawyer, doctor specializing in surgery, etc. Or any position related to the science of Gandharva Veda (primal music therapy).

Mercury = Crown Prince: All fields involving teaching and communication or bartering and trading. Or any career related to astrology or mathematics.

Jupiter = Minister: All dignified ministerial positions such as banker, judge, priest, college professor, psychologist, politician, company executive, etc. Or any position where a sense of selfless service and giving are prerequisites. Or also any position related to the science of priestly ritual (Kalpa).

Venus = Minister: All dignified ministerial positions which have either an artistic or scientific bent, such as horticulturist, nutritionist, bee keeper, designer, decorator, painter, musician, etc. Or any career related to the science of geomancy.

Saturn = Servant: Practical, logical, mundane, "hands-on" types of work such as plumber, miner, computer specialist, technician, philosophical logician, manual laborer, etc. Or any career related to health science (Ayurveda) which is practical and down to earth like massage therapy, physical therapy, chiropractic, etc.

Nodes of the Moon = Foot-soldiers: Careers which allow a person to be rebellious, anti-establishment, and iconoclastic.

When we are young, the planet governing our creative play nature may affect our career choice, especially if the planet governing career is weak. As we mature, the planet governing career becomes increasingly influential in our work habits.

Those who have the Nodes of the Moon governing career nature are best as independent consultants where their originality, individuality, insight, and imaginative vision is valued and sought out.

Those whose career natures are under the influence of the Sun have trouble settling on one career. Most careers are not multi-faceted enough to suit them. Solar-types like to LEAD!

Saturn-types will often take on a tough job that no one else wants to tackle. They bring order to any chaos through their methodical organizing skills.

Mercurial-types hate jobs where there is no variety. They love jobs that involve change.

Mars-types are good at motivating other people into taking action. They mobilize the will!

Venus is very good in careers which require the skills of compromise and peace-making. They like to see the beautiful in everything and are very positive and optimistic in their approach.

Jupiter-types bring a spirit of selfless service and giving to their work. They also have a balanced approach to anything they do.

Lunar-types like jobs where they can be surrogate mothers.

Fortunate indeed are those individuals who have a stable, productive, and satisfying career.

I know a person whose dharma is Shudra, the servant caste, and whose career nature is governed by Mars. She is very effective in her career of counseling people on their spiritual and life paths, serving them by motivating their will to take action for their own self-improvement and betterment in life. So you see how fluid these general categories can be. They are not to be taken too literally or defined too rigidly.

If the planet governing a person's career nature is weak and/or poorly placed, all the professional career counseling in the world will fail to adequately resolve the matter. The person affected must understand that this weakness exists and must therefore, avoid placing an inordinate emphasis on goals related to this field of living. It is not about the goal, but about the activity itself.

For most people income is derived from their careers. When the career nature is weak, the person may change jobs too often or hold on to a job too long. In either case, income tends to suffer.

How well we hold on to the money we have earned is determined from another field of living: wealth, or primal desire nature.

Saturn: Systematic, logical, practical, orderly, detail-oriented careers.

Venus: Among Brahmins, Venus governs careers related to counseling. When one is a Shudra or craftsperson, Venus governs artistic endeavors. When one is a Vaishya or member of the business caste, Venus governs business endeavors with an artistic component. Alternatively, one can be an empirical scientist or biologist. Such people are also good in mediation and arbitration because of their peace-making skills.

Mars: Supervisory skills are ruled by Mars. Those who have Mars governing their career nature also make good motivational speakers and counselors.

Moon: When the Moon relates to one's career nature, it indicates nourishing, mothering-type professions such as nursing.

Mercury: Mercury loves to communicate, to teach, to write, to express itself.

Jupiter: Jupiterian beings enjoy careers filled with abundant rewards, prestige, honor, and dignity. They are good as bankers, senators, judges, professors, counselors, or any other position where the ability to give sound, balanced advice is valued and handsomely remunerated.

Sun: The Sun is a true entrepreneur, whether in art, science, or religion.

The Sun is always ahead of its time. When its influence is directly related to any artistic, scientific, or religious creation, that creation is slow to be recognized, because it is so avant-garde.

The Sun is the perfect commander-in-chief, or physician.

When the Sun rules career but is weak , a dictator may be born.

Rahu/Ketu: If the Nodes of the Moon govern the career nature, then the person should either work for himself, or find a career where his break-out-of-the-matrix nature is valued by his employers.

Creative Play
The Field of Recreation

This describes how we re-create, how we enjoy ourselves, our creative gifts and also determines our relationship with children (our own or others'). Each planet describes a different style of play.

Sun: Charismatic, liberal, authoritative, confident
Moon: Caring, nourishing, loving, empathetic
Mars: Courageous, assertive, challenging, and willing to take risks
Mercury: Flexible, adaptable, discerning, verbal, and changeable
Jupiter: Fair, just, highly social, moderate, and altruistic
Venus: Soft, sweet, compromising, positive, idealistic, and socially minded
Saturn: Disciplined, patient, slow, retiring and dependable, especially in times of crises, basking
Nodes of the Moon: Rebellious, iconoclastic, independent

The field of creative play is concerned with play, how we refresh ourselves when not obliged to be serious. How we play, how we recreate, how we enjoy ourselves when not performing worldly duties, is dictated by this field of living.

This field of living also determines our relationship with children (our own or others'). When we have a strong play nature, then it is enjoyable and fun to be with children. Otherwise it is a burden.

Children want nothing more than a playful attentiveness from adults. In this sense child-rearing can be easy, but only if one has a strong play nature.

There are eight major styles of creative play, corresponding to the seven major planets plus the Nodes of the Moon. How we best express our creative aptitudes depends not only on the creative gift itself, but also on our dharma (caste nature) and career nature (success and influence).

Mercury governs speech, writing, and communication. If Mercury rules your creative gifts and your caste nature is Brahmin, then you probably enjoy teaching and dealing with higher knowledge, and you are likely to be very good as a teacher, priest, or counselor. However, if your creative gifts are ruled by Mercury and your dharma is the Vaishya (merchant) class, then you more likely enjoy negotiating and trading, making business a form of play.

The expression of our creative gifts is also affected by our career nature. For example, a publisher with Venusian creative gifts might deal in romance novels or idealistic books, while a publisher with Saturnine creative gifts would prefer detailed, technically oriented nonfiction.

Our creative gifts affect both our work and our play. What is your favorite recreation? Saturn likes solitude and quiet, Mars likes aggressive sports and competition, Venus likes idealistic romance, etc.

Children are a major expression of our creativity. If the planet ruling our creative gifts is weak or afflicted, we are unlikely to have children, or our children are likely to have difficulties. If our play nature is weak, then we can become overly attached to having children, and once we have them, we can also be overly possessive of them.

People with weak play natures get very tired and stressed. They do not know how to regenerate and restore themselves (re-creation) through play.

A crisis requires a creative solution; creativity and a sense of play go hand in hand. Thus, those with weak play natures often respond poorly to crisis. They fall apart.

Some people can turn their play nature into a source of lucrative income as demonstrated by many professional athletes.

Each planet demonstrates a different style of play. This style can be applied to how the person recreates, or what he enjoys as recreation, and his attitude towards and relationship with his children.

When the planet governing the creative play nature is weak or malefic, then it can create the following in one's role as a parent or playmate:

- The Sun: dictatorial, arrogant, "know-it-all"
- The Moon: cruel, withholds love as punishment
- Mars: hateful, jealous, envious, aggressive, combative
- Mercury: too changeable, verbose, serious or self-preoccupied; likes to expose the flaws of others
- Jupiter: extravagance, dissipation, over-protectiveness, and rigid application of ideals
- Venus: too demanding of affection, unrealistic expectations regarding romance and friendship
- Saturn: very controlling, especially in regard to privacy issues
- Nodes of the Moon: criminal activity, anti-social revolutionary behavior

Mars enjoys risk-taking forms of play.

Mercury likes quickly moving, ever-changing, more cerebral forms of play.

The Sun will only enjoy a form of play organized, led, or decided upon by the Sun.

Venus enjoys cooperative forms of play, rather than highly competitive ones. Its form of social interaction is more light and superficial when compared to that of Jupiter.

The role of motherhood can be a most natural activity – as well as a great joy – when the Moon or Jupiter governs the play nature.

When the Nodes govern the play nature, the person often relates with his children in an iconoclastic manner; he gives his children the same privilege however.

A Saturnine parent can often be quite emotionally distant towards the children, even though he feels guilty about it at times.

When the planet governing the play nature temporarily rules at any particular time in the life, it is a good time to "kick-back" and relax, to creatively brainstorm about where one has been and where one might like to go. It is not a good time for carrying out orderly, methodical regimens or routines in any of the other seven fields of living.

Can one learn how to play?

Most creative insights come after we have let go of the problem and our determination to solve it.

If you can go to the very brink of sleep, to the transition point between waking and sleeping, while maintaining a conscious awareness of a problem needing to be solved, the answer will be there when you awaken.

All solutions flower when we let go of the idea that we alone can solve them.

This is the field of living that governs the way we play, the way we recreate, and the way we "hang out", either by ourselves or with others. It is what we do when we have no other duties and responsibilities to perform. It is how we entertain ourselves.

And, since the creation of children is also part of this field of living, it also determines our relationship with children, and whether we choose to even have children.

If the planet governing this field of living is strong, then we entertain ourselves and others well. If it is weak, then we are in trouble to some extent.

Place two people together who both have this field of living weak, and you end up with two uncomfortable people. Or vice versa if their planets are strong.

Each planet gives a different style of play. Saturn, for example, makes us content with quiet, simple physical types of recreation and play – taking a walk, or just relaxing. Mars would give a more risk-taking disposition to the forms of play.

Saturn: If Saturn governs creative play, the person needs very little stimulus in order to enjoy himself; it may be a long walk, a cup of tea, or just some silent time on the porch. With children they will either be a little shy and remote, and/or very controlling. The patriarchal, fundamentalist preacher who demands that his children "toe the line" is a good example of an overly Saturnine reaction.

Venus: One's children are seen in a most positive and favorable light when Venus governs the creative play nature. Thus, they tend to grow up with high self-esteem. If Venus is weak, however, the parent will be overly indulgent. The child will be spoiled.

Mars: A play nature ruled by Mars requires adventure and risk. One's avocation might be jumping motorcycles over obstacles, bungee jumping, etc.

154

Moon: When the Moon governs the field of creative play, then raising children becomes a joyful avocation, as well as a necessary vocation.

Mercury: Mercury's creative play with both children and adults tends to be through deep communication and/or through word games or puns. Thus, Mercury tends to play better with children who have reached the age of reason.

Jupiter: When Jupiter governs the field of creative play, then raising children and interacting with them is a great joy, rather than a duty or somber responsibility.

Sun: Loves to play in ways that showcase themselves, with them at the center of attention, onstage, or in the spotlight. Authoritative in relation to children.

Rahu/Ketu: Their relationship to children will be equally rebellious and iconoclastic, and their forms of play will shock others – either humorously or maddeningly.

Mental Health
The Field of the Vital Body

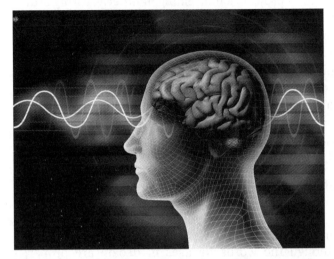

This field is an indication of the energy we project into the world which is often referred to as our personality. This field is also known as our Vital Body, or our vitality.

When we think of mental health, two different aspects come to mind:

- stress management
- emotional balance

Stress management involves the vital body; emotional balance involves the emotional body. These are two separate sheaths in the human being; however, they are usually treated together under the designation of mental health.

Although there is a relationship between the two, we need to differentiate between them. Someone can be quite tense and overly sensitive yet still be emotionally balanced – at least this is my suggestion to you.

A strong vital body gives individuals the energy and ability to creatively project themselves into any environment. One tends to be successful and influential because of this ability. Abraham Lincoln had a powerful energy body and nothing could deter him from achieving his objective.

When a person wants to project his energy onto the environment in a way that will bring success, influence, popularity, and good reputation, then he will use one of eight styles for doing so:

- The Sun projects charismatic leadership
- The Moon projects a nourishing, motherly, caring attitude
- Mars projects competence, courage, confidence, and assertiveness
- Mercury projects adaptability, flexibility, and a keen, perceptive intelligence
- Jupiter projects joyfulness, moderation, balance, tolerance, and altruism
- Venus projects peace, harmony, and positivity
- Saturn projects steadiness, patience, and dependability
- Nodes of the Moon project rebelliousness, iconoclasm, individualism, and independence

One must learn to distinguish between a person's relating style and the manner in which he projects his energy onto the environment. For example, one famous author, political commentator, and debater has a Jupiterian relating style and a Martian way of projecting his energy field. Thus, although the words he uses in debate are proper, polite and civilized, the underlying tone is quite combative.

Mental health is how we project ourselves, the energy behind our actions in the world. It has a direct effect on our fame and public image.

Even in the prevailing Western model, mental health is largely a matter of how others perceive us. One lady who has spent over a quarter century in mental hospitals has a debilitated Mercury ruling this field. As a teenager, she was bright, charming, a good student, and talented in music and drama. But the weak Mercury left her devoid of common sense, preoccupied with others' opinion of her, and powerless to express herself verbally.

The Ayurvedic model of ancient India offers a less morbid view of the mind than the Western psychotherapeutic model. Ayurveda teaches that the universe is the interplay of three opposing forces, or gunas, and that each individual can find a point of balance between the opposing forces. There are three basic types of mental constitution corresponding to the three:

Sattwic: Calm, pure, harmonizing, and inclined toward upright behavior and the pursuit of truth

Rajasic: Driven by material desires, such as wealth, power, sensuality, or anything exciting

Tamasic: Lazy, indolent, careless, and dull-minded

Within each of these broad types there are many gradations and subtypes. Different areas of the mind also display different tendencies. One may have a very sattwic attitude toward reading scriptures every day, a rajasic attitude toward competition in a cutthroat business, and an indolent, tamasic attitude toward preparing one's tax returns. Nevertheless, one of the three tendencies tends to dominate one's mental activity.

A sattwic disposition is conducive to meditation and spiritual pursuits. It also promotes mental and physical health and heals disease tendencies developed from rajasic or tamasic habits.

A strong spiritual nature often compensates for a weak mental nature, so that one is able to function adequately in society in spite of a lack in confidence. However, if both the mental and spiritual natures are weak, the result is usually mental illness, criminal behavior, or at least a tendency for poor decisions which seriously undermine the quality of life.

The best antidote for any weakness in this field is a spiritual regimen in accord with one's natural path of spirituality. The various yogas and tantra, properly practiced, have a profound effect on all aspects of our life. Hundreds of studies have shown the benefits of Transcendental Meditation (TM) in relieving stress. More research is needed on other techniques, and the different effects of various meditation practices. We believe that the results are greatest when one practices in accord with one's own spiritual nature.

How we play and how we care for our bodies also affect our mental health. The ancient masters of Ayurveda saw that mental illness is often just a symptom of physical imbalance, and vice versa. By treating the physical cause, such as a blood-sugar imbalance, the behavior frequently corrects itself.

Our lasting reputation is very much determined by this field of living and the strength of the planet governing it.

Those individuals who have a weak vital body display some of the following characteristics:

- Shyness in public
- Procrastination
- Inability to keep one's immediate surroundings orderly

- Difficulty in projecting oneself
- A poor public image or reputation
- Feeling that one is "spinning one's wheels" to achieve success
- Feeling unduly stressed from stimuli with others
- Feeling that one must constantly retreat to avoid the pressures of the world

Maharishi Mahesh Yogi was one of the first Eastern sages to point out the nature of stress and to offer simple meditative techniques for dealing with it. Hans Selye was one of the first Western scientists to isolate and study the phenomena of stress.

Raja Yoga is an effective stress management tool because of its intimate relationship to Venus and the vital body.

Aerobics is a Western modality for dealing with stress. However, some sages suggest that excessive aerobic activity saps one's vitality and can actually shorten the life span.

As we become more crowded in our living and work space, stress accumulates!

Geomancy is the science of ordering the environment to minimize and virtually eliminate stress.

Those who are gifted with artistic sensibilities are naturally attuned to the fundamental principles of geomancy.

Dr. Bach, who created the Bach Flower Remedies, understood the seven basic negative emotional tendencies: pride, cruelty, hate, self-infatuation, rigid or misplaced loyalties, procrastination, and insecurity/control issues. Certain Bach flower remedies can also be used to alleviate certain negative mental health tendencies.

Each person will have one of eight styles or methods of resolving emotions. No one method will work for everyone and no one method is superior to the others; individual suitability is the key. Your Spiritual Blueprint identifies which planet governs the emotions, and consequently, which style of therapy is most appropriate for that individual. For example, if Mars governs the emotions, then the person will often benefit by challenging himself with risk-taking adventures such as those offered by Outward Bound. Rational Emotive Therapy is useful for individuals who have Mercury governing their emotional nature. If Saturn governs the emotions, the person is soothed through seclusion, breath and bodywork.

It is important to distinguish the field of mental health from physical health problems which cause mental health imbalances. Otherwise, you won't get to the root of the problem. For example, if someone suffers from depression, they may go through years of psychotherapy to treat it only to find out that the depression has a physical cause.

The opposite may also be true. Someone may be trying to find a physical cause for mental health problems and be frustrated because the problem is actually a mental one.

There is an intimate relationship between geomancy, or Sthapatya Veda, and the field of mental health. The most important strategy in mental health care is to create the proper environment for mental health (freedom from undue stress) and happiness.

Each planet governs a particular type of environment:

Sun: temples and holy places, and places where one feels like a king in one's environment. Also, sunny places, and the East.

Moon: watery, cool, nourishing places such as exist in the Northwest part of the United States. Places where "mother is at home", or the motherland.

Mars: warm, fiery places where there is a strong, warrior ethic such as in the Southern U.S.

Mercury: intellectually stimulating places where there are many different things to do such as in big cities. Or where there are many recreational opportunities. Mercury rules the North.

Jupiter: places of wealth, power, and prestige such as large cities like New York City and Washington, D.C. Also, places where family values are upheld, such as the towns of the northeast.

Venus: places in the Southeast like Florida where there is fun, surf, beauty, romance and parties.

Rahu: the Southwest, where people can be rebels, and where being different is a way of life.

You can expand upon these brief descriptions by studying the significations of each planet and relating them to the environment.

Since a different planet governs mental health for each person, one of the important parts of mental health counseling is to identify the right environment for each person.

Each planet also governs a negative emotion:

Sun: pride

Moon: cruelty or the withholding of love

Mars: hatred and jealousy

Mercury: self-love and preoccupation

Jupiter: rigid thinking and attachment to certain values

Venus: scattered thinking, procrastination, and lack of control over the senses

Saturn: insecurity and fear, and over-control of others

This implies that the planet ruling mental health also causes excesses which become mental health problems. So the planet defines not only the ideal environment for us, but also how excesses in such an environment breed mental health problems.

Saturn: If a person is under great stress and has Saturn governing his mental health, he needs a lot of quiet time and privacy to fully recover his mental and emotional equilibrium.

Venus: When Venus governs mental health, the person has the capacity to turn on the Venusian charm in order to be successful and influential with others. Others may tend to view him as positive, peaceful, and harmonious, even when he is not actually this way.

If you watch a porpoise play in the surf, you will get a feeling for what it feels like when Venus governs the vital body. Or listen or dance to a Strauss waltz to feel this energy.

Mars: When Mars governs the vital body, the person displays a strong, willful, courageous, daring nature.

Moon: A strong lunar mental health nature indicates that a person is capable of projecting a compassionate, empathetic quality to achieve his or her goals. Whether the person actually is compassionate is determined by an examination of other key fields of living.

Mercury: When Mercury governs the vital body, the person shows up as a quick-witted, fast-paced thinker who will finish your sentences.

Jupiter: When Jupiter governs the energy body, then the person gives the impression of being moderate, balanced, and pure (*sattwic*) in everything he does. He projects an energy field strongly influenced by Jupiter.

Sun: The Sun displays boundless energy until one gets overheated.

Rahu/Ketu: A person whose mental health is ruled by the Nodes of the Moon tends to rebel against traditional methods for dealing with stress. He finds his own unique, and even sometimes shocking methods for dealing with his own mental health.

Physical Health
The Field of the Physical Body

Edward has written an entire book about this field, *Ayurveda Revolutionized: Integrating Ancient and Modern Ayurveda*. To summarize:

A holistic study of physical health is also multi-dimensional with seven basic body types, seven tissue elements, seven major organ systems, and seven forms of therapeutics. And each of the seven major planets defines one component of each aspect of holistic health.

Sun: disease of heat, bone tissue, heart organ, and fomentation therapy. The Sun governs the bones, the heart and the disease of heat. When the Sun governs physical health, the person wants to be his own physician.

Moon: disease of coldness, blood tissue, brain, and cooling therapy

Jupiter: disease of heaviness, fat tissue, liver, and nourishing therapy

Mars: disease of lightness, marrow tissue, gall bladder, and lightening therapy

Venus: disease of oiliness, reproductive tissue, kidneys, sex organs and pancreas, and oleation therapy

Saturn: disease of dryness, muscle tissue, spleen, and astringent or drying therapy

Mercury: mixed disease, lymph tissue, lungs, and mixed therapy.

Nodes of the Moon: diseases through one of the seven major planets as well as diseases which are difficult to diagnose and treat through traditional treatments, since they are directly due to past-life influences.

Edward's book, *Ayurveda Revolutionized: Integrating Ancient and Modern Ayurveda,* (also published by Lotus Press) contains many case histories of people who respond well to the multifaceted therapeutics of his archetypal, planetary Ayurveda, often after years of frustration with other approaches.

Chapter 9
Some Conditions that
May Contribute to Awakening

Awakening may appear as a spontaneous realization, a recognition, of who one is, of who one has always been. It often comes suddenly, though often this sudden awakening has been preceded by years or lifetimes of spiritual preparation. Whether the clouds suddenly part or dissipate gradually, the Sun will shine through.

The awakening of an individual to his/her true universal nature seems to occur along with similar, apparently contributing conditions that seem to favor or perhaps create the initial conditions for a ripe field for Awakening to occur.

These are:

- The occurrence of traumatic emotional events in a person's life or the fear of these events.

- The desire for Liberation, usually an intense, passionate desire. Sometimes this desire takes the form of an intense desire to know God, or a deep longing.

- A spiritual Guru or teacher, embodied or disembodied, animate or inanimate.

This teacher, even though inanimate or disembodied, may contribute to a person's awakening in these ways:

- Gives the experience of thoughts subsiding or dissolving so that pure Awareness can shine forth.

- Dissolves the fixation on Appearance rather than Substance, on form as opposed to Awareness, facilitating discrimination between the Real (ever-present Awareness) and the Unreal (the changing field of phenomena).

- Abandonment of all attachments.

- Moment-to-moment immersion in the Self (a.k.a. Surrender).

Traumatic Events

It seems, perhaps even often, the occurrence of traumatic events precedes one's Awakening.

What is a traumatic event? People experience events and circumstances as traumatic when they have a mental picture of how they desperately want the circumstances to look and then the circumstances don't look that way. A traumatic event might be a near-death experience; the sudden death of a loved one; the sudden loss of a job, money, or economic self-sufficiency; divorce; loss of social status; or a sudden illness or injury. Not to mention wars, mass executions, starvation, earthquakes, hurricanes, tornadoes, floods, droughts, murders, rapes, maimings, and all manner of horrors. Most people experience these events as devastating, as intensely painful, emotionally and sometimes physically.

In other words, life. Circumstances of life here on planet Earth are generally traumatic from time to time. We certainly don't need to go looking for them. They seem to present themselves in abundance.

And sometimes, perhaps often, these traumatic circumstances of life can bring about the demise of the one experiencing them. However, some times, through some act of grace, if the emotions that accompany these events are met fully, are experienced fully, the story, the mental spinning and fear that accompany them, can fall away. Or at least dissipate enough for the silent stillness at the core of all Being to come through.

But even though a traumatic event may be an intense experience, often the fear alone that a traumatic event will or might occur is sufficient to 'trigger' awakening. Many times this fear is an even more powerful trigger than the actual occurrence of the traumatic event itself. It may not be anything in particular about an event itself that creates the trauma, but rather an individual's mental/emotional response to the event that contains the power to bring the mind to its knees.

As Marianne Williamson has said, "A nervous breakdown is a highly underrated method of spiritual awakening."

Ramana Maharishi's awakening occurred after his beloved uncle's death and his facing the terror of his own mortality. In this experience, he realized what dies and what cannot.

Saul of Tarsus, St. Paul, experienced his awakening on the road to Damascus while riding his horse after having persecuted and martyred hundreds, perhaps thousands, of Christians.

Beethoven and Buckminster Fuller are two other examples of people who at their moment of ultimate despair and imminent suicide, report that they turned over their lives to humanity, became servants of something much bigger than their individual selves. And it was only after this point in their lives that they began to express their true authentic nature.

What is it about traumatic occurrences that make them significant in many Awakenings?

Perhaps it is the intense emotions that accompany such events and the disruption of the mind-numbing influence of our life routines. The realization of the fragility and temporary nature of life.Traumatic events are such sudden, dramatic phenomenon and may be experienced with such a degree of intensity... the intensity of this experience has the power to break through the veneer of mental conditioning in which people live from day to day. A traumatic event may give rise to deep, existential despair, to introspection, and create an opening to the Big Picture, or a search for meaning or understanding of the purpose of one's existence.

But more importantly, sometimes, when used appropriately, when faced directly, the intense energy of these emotions has the power to break the mental boundaries of conditioned existence. The intense emotions they evoke can break through the cloud of mental conditioning, the conceptual framework of one's life. They can annihilate the mind.

Desire for Awakening

An intense desire to awaken also seems to contribute. This desire may take any number of forms, such as the desire to know God, or the desire to be free from suffering, or the intense desire for liberation. This intense desire can be triggered and fueled by traumatic events.

The desire for Awakening, even though it may be weak at first, can produce "results." But the results seem to be much slower and less far-reaching than when the desire is strong. When the desire becomes the dominant force, it may be experienced as an intense longing. When this longing is faced fully, it finally has the power to consume one's whole being. This intense desire, when faced fully, can annihilate the mind (temporarily).

What is the benefit of having one's mind temporarily flattened? What remains is pure Awareness. The experience of pure awareness as who one is allows for the discovery that the mind, all thoughts, arise within it. This experience can cut the identification with the mind. In other words, it can expand one's experience of him/her self from being identified with a particular personality and mindstream. The personality and thoughts that occur then begin to be seen as the role that one plays, like the suit of clothes that one wears (though not one that can be 'changed' quite so easily).

An East Indian story illustrates the importance of intense desire to facilitate awakening. One day, so the story goes, a Guru and his disciple were in a boat on a lake, when the disciple asked, "How greatly must a man desire God to Realize Him?"

The Guru then threw the disciple out of the boat into the water and held him, head and all, beneath the surface until the disciple was close to inhaling water. Then, drawing the disciple into the boat, the Guru asked, "What was it that you desired while under the water?"

The disciple gasped, "Air, air, air!"

Then, the Guru said, "When you desire God as intensely as you just now desired air, then you will find Him!"

The Role of the Guru

The third condition that may contribute to awakening for some people is the Presence of a Guru, or spiritual teacher.

What is the Guru? The appearance in another form of one's own Self. Though the *satguru* appears in everything at all times, calling one home to his/her own Self, the Guru is the specific manifestation in form of the satguru, the formless, genderless, inductive energy of Presence that has the power to dissipate the mind.

In truth, there is only one Guru. It is the timeless Self, pure Awareness. And the Self appears in numerous forms in time, from time to time.

The Guru, or spiritual teacher, need not necessarily appear in human form, though it usually does. The Guru might appear embodied or disembodied, animate or inanimate. Ramana Maharishi's guru was Mt. Arunachula which he experienced as a manifestation of Shiva, pure Presence.

One knows a true Guru, one's spiritual teacher, when in the Presence of the Guru the mind of the student is stopped. And occasionally, blessedly, the boundaries between the Guru and his disciple become so blurred, that all individual differences in form are perceived as superficial. The Guru is thus perceived as the appearance in form of one's own Self, as the same Self which animates one's own body also moving through and animating the Guru's body, much as the same Self moves one's own arm while not being separate from the arm.

Many may be familiar with appearances of the Guru in human form. It is often said that the Guru is so empty (of mind) that one can see one's own Self in him. The satguru can manifest in innumerable forms simultaneously. To some it may need to appear as an East Indian monk to be recognized. To others it might appear as a white American woman from the South. To others it might appear as a mountain, or an ocean, or in the writings or teachings or presence of a person no longer inhabiting a human form, as a saint, an avatar, an angel, or messianic manifestation. All serve to break apart the veil of individual separate existence, though different manifestations of the same Self may resonate with different individuals in a way that speaks to – and subsequently annihilates – their minds.

The Guru even though inanimate or disembodied, contributes to the following occurrences:

Gives the experience of Freedom.

- Dissolves the fixation on Appearance rather than Substance, on form as opposed to Awareness, facilitating discrimination between the Real and the Unreal.

- Abandonment of all attachments.

- Moment-to-moment immersion in the Self (a.k.a. Surrender).

Of course, we must always use our power of discrimination, of discernment, to know when we are being served, and when we are giving our power away to another. By being true to our Self, we will know when we are being served. We should never give our power away to an other.

However, we will be served by giving up all thought to total surrender of each and every thought in this moment. Only when the Presence of the Guru facilitates this dissipation of the mind is s/he of value. Only when the Guru is perceived as no other, is s/he to be followed, for then we are only following our own Self. As has often been said, "If you see the Buddha in the road, kill him", meaning, the true Buddha is inside, and if he appears as another, then this is a false guru.

The problem with following a Guru is that it can perpetuate the same old tendency of the mind to find its fulfillment in an "other", to be outer-directed. Awakening occurs when the mind does an about face and becomes inner-directed. Seated in the Self, all thought emerges as the energetic phenomena they are, insubstantial, fleeting, ephemeral.

The Experience of Freedom

Before Awakening can be desired, it must be sensed or felt, either strongly or faintly, as desirable. The Presence of those who have already Awakened, together with their testimony regarding their Realization, may give a person an indication that there is something Beyond which he has been longing for, providing fuel to the fire of that longing. An Awakened Guru, by his Presence and testimony, will fan the flame of this fire, throwing the student headlong into the fire of his own longing.

The Presence of the Guru is always helpful. This Presence has variously been called "darshan", "grace", and "transmission". To be in the energy field, in the embodied Presence, of One who has lost all identification, is to be in a field of Consciousness which tends to arouse within the individual some degree of the corresponding level of Consciousness. An empathic, or energetic, entrainment can occur. In physics, *resonance* is a phenomenon that occurs when a vibrating system or external force drives another system to oscillate with greater amplitude at a specific preferential frequency. This higher vibrational frequency, emanations of Grace, can elevate the consciousness of anyone in his/her field, and have the effect of silencing the mind.

From this point of view if we regard Consciousness as emanations of a certain kind of Energy analogous to certain properties of electricity, Consciousness may be experienced as transmitted or induced in the student. This reception may be slight or of any degree up to one of high intensity. The transmission tends to dissipate the hardened or congealed energy of the mind, with the possibility of subsequently annihilating it totally for a moment or some moments.

172

After the removal of the presence of the inducing Consciousness, the glow of the induced Consciousness may persist for a longer or shorter time. But repeated exposure, repeated inductions, tend, finally, to produce a condition such that the Inner Light of the individual is aroused sympathetically into pulsation and thus, ultimately, "catches on." This is the report of many who have met their true Guru. When this happens, the individual has for the first time become established in his own Center in the higher sense. He becomes One grounded in the Higher Light, instead of being merely a student.

This induction/transmission is an enormous instrument for effecting Awakening. Those who aspire to Awaken would do well to seize every opportunity available to come within the sphere of those who can serve as such Centers of induction.

This effect may be most pronounced in those whose primary spiritual path is the path of Bhakti, the path of Selfless Service, or the Integral path, though others may benefit as well.

Dissolving the Illusion of Form

The more Awakened Ones encountered and truly met, the better. Even if the seeker continues for a time to be caught up in the outward grasping mind, looking outside one's self for that which one seeks, Being in the Presence of numerous Awakened Beings affords the opportunity for the individual to transcend the form of Awakening and see what lies beyond the individual form, the stillness at the core. And subsequently to recognize that that stillness is 'Who I am.'

Meeting numerous forms of the Awakened One also enables a person to know that Others, who are like him/herself, have Awakened and to know that Awakening is possible for him/her too.

The aphorism, "When the pupil is ready, the Teacher will appear," makes it clear that the student need not seek far and wide in distant lands for someone to take him under their direction. The Guru can, and does, appear in an inward sense, often without the individual mind being aware of it. When the desire for Awakening is sufficiently strong, all of the forces of the universe seem to marshall their support to come to its aid.

Sometimes the Guru may appear outwardly in human form. And again, the Guru may or may not be recognized at first. Even though a person cannot command the Guru or summon him forth, he will appear when the call is made earnestly, for His/Hers is a service of Love and in Love. S/He serves only Love. And His/Her will, the awakening of all Being, cannot inevitably be denied. So, in effect, the student by doing his/her part, by facing the intense longing of her/his soul, the desire for Freedom, for Awakening, does participate in invoking the aid s/he needs.

And the individual mind does need the support, the assistance, of that which is beyond all mind but which has the power to annihilate the mind. The power and presence of Shiva, the grand annihilator, is ever present to sever the head, to bring all form including mind form, to its knees. He need only be invoked, invited in. And he will take charge. Do not be confused by anthropomorphic descriptions (e.g., Shiva). Shiva is a powerful force that can silence our minds.

This natural release of the mind back to its source that is so effortlessly evoked in the recognition of Who One Is, at times may seem to be personal, at times impersonal. In fact, and experience, it is beyond the realm of personal and impersonal.

The importance of the Guru lies in the fact that Awakening is not an effect of any cause set up in the space-time or subject-object, relative, ever-changing sphere of life. That which transcends causality cannot be Itself an effect of some cause. Awakening is a spontaneous induction of Awareness Itself. What can be done, perhaps, with the assistance of a Guru or the support of Others, is to remove "barriers" that inhibit this spontaneous induction.

Even if one who desires Awakening has not established a personal relationship with a Guru such that direct outer instruction is possible, then relationship with and merging into the Guru may be attained through embracing the words and works of the Awakened Ones who either are now living in physical bodies or have lived in the past and have left their visible signs. The Illumined One is actually present in His works, in His speech and His writings.

The writings of a Self-Realized One are not merely symbols or concepts. They are the embodiments of a living Presence which is actually Self as manifested through the particular Self-Realized One who wrote them.

A serious aspirant would be well-advised to peruse the writings and sayings of as many Awakened Ones as possible, until he finds one that resonates with him. Because not all aspects of the Divine Manifestation are equally accessible to all, that which works for one is not necessarily what will work for another. Realization manifests in a vast range of forms, some seemingly the opposite of others, so all beings may be served in the easiest and most direct Way. When the student has found One with whose Words and Consciousness s/he stands in particularly close

174

rapport, s/he should then delve deeply into that One's writings and sayings.

These writings may only be of real value if they produce the effect of the annihilation of the mind and the revelation of Self. Writings taken on an intellectual level can serve as further obstacles to that which is sought, the annihilation of the mind.

It is not merely the conceptual value of the words of the Awakened Ones that is important. Their expressions may well not be the best possible for any individual. But surrounding and within the words is the real Message which has the transformative power. It is this more or less veiled Message that should be embraced without resistance, the inductive energy contained and expressed by the words.

Invariably the teaching of the true Guru, his words, will point the student in the direction of the Self, that which is Real and unchanging. The Guru may then guide the student through the use of the discriminative faculty, the intellect, in differentiating between that which is changing (thought, emotion, sense perception) and that which is unchanging (Self, silent Awareness, Source). This is the path of the intellect, the path of the Gyan Yogi, and is an approach that is especially useful for those whose spiritual nature is governed by this path. Shankara's *Crest Jewel of Discrimination* is the classic example of this teaching. This fundamental teaching appears over and over in and from various forms, expressed in different ways.

Abandonment of Attachments

As Jesus said, it is easier for a rich man to pass through the eye of a needle than for him to enter the kingdom of heaven. The poor, meek, and humble shall inherit the kingdom.

What is meant by these sayings is not necessarily that one must be without money, so much as that one may only Awaken when he is unencumbered with mental riches and emotional baggage, unattached. It is helpful to approach the spiritual search with an open mind, free of resistances, and earnestly. An attitude of open inquiry, of truly investigating and opening to the effects that any particular spiritual path has to offer, putting aside one's skeptical mind for just one moment, is an important prerequisite to fully receiving the gifts offered by each spiritual path.

"Unencumbered" does not mean that the mind and emotions are not there. It simply means that the individual is not identified with them, he is "unencumbered" by them, awareness is not obscured. The occurrence of tragic or intensely dramatic circumstances in one's life can establish the initial conditions for Awakening, creating a humbling of the mind, and a realization that 'I am not in control'; that there are "forces of nature" that are bigger and more powerful than my limited, individual mind can control, that I cannot always make things look the way I want.

Traumatic circumstances set the stage for the deepest kind of surrender: surrender of the mind in every moment to its creator, to its source, to the silence/stillness at the core. They provide the opportunity for the mind to be humbled, to give up its attempts to control the circumstances, the environment and what one calls "my life."

Jesus's sayings also imply that the outer-directedness, the grasping, commonly attributed to those with financial wealth, can be a significant obstacle to one's realization of the kingdom of heaven within. Perhaps because a person with financial resources has so much success in fulfilling his desires with money, his wealth contributes to his continuing to look outside himself, externally, for what he really wants.

Of course, this is not just a condition of a rich person, but tends to be the widespread condition of virtually the entire human race. We think that what we want can be had through the fulfillment of desires. As each desire is fulfilled, it produces some moment or moments of satisfaction or contentment. Rich people have quite a bit of success in fulfilling their desires, or at least they may not have much of a financial obstacle to doing so. Generally what happens is that their desires just seem to get bigger and bigger. So their minds can very easily be caught in the outward projection of continuous, never-ending feeding and satiating of desires. All that may be required is for a Guru to point the way off of this mind spin, this continuous cycle of desire and desire fulfillment.

But if a person has very little success fulfilling his desires, he has the opportunity to stop looking to the fulfillment of desires for the fulfillment s/he craves. He has the opportunity to get off of the never-ending cycle of desire and to recognize the pure Awareness in which all desire arises.

Of course, the circumstances of Buddha ran contrary to this model. Buddha awoke to the Truth of his Being having begun as a Prince with all the worldly possessions and comforts anyone could ever hope for. In the midst of his incredible wealth he realized that his possessions and comforts did not give him what he truly longed for, and he gave them all up. He awoke sitting under the Bodhi tree in the midst of and meeting the most spectacular display of mind-created phenomenal temptation.

So, it is not necessarily the case that a poor man has a decided advantage so much as that he may have one less obstacle. It does seem to be easier for one to give up his addiction to pain than it is to give up his attachment to pleasure. In truth, poor people and rich people are both seemingly equally hopelessly lost in the same struggle, the seemingly never-ending quest of desire fulfillment.

The Guru can assist by helping to break the mental boundaries, conceptual paradigms, and value systems of his aspirants, loosening the grip of the mind. One way he does this is by repeated contradictions, inconsistencies, and thoroughly unpredictable, spontaneous behavior and words which disallow the student from abidance in the mind. It is imperative that the student realize that Awakening is not an understanding that can be grasped by the mind, but the moment-to-moment Presence of his own Self. For this realization, often the disallowance of any concept on which the mind can alight and make its own is required.

None of the foregoing is in any way intended to imply that the Guru willfully creates conditions which lack the stability and consistency of a person's seemingly normal conditioned existence. It is simply his nature to be totally spontaneous and responsive to the needs and energetic phenomena which present themselves in any given moment. The Guru is the embodiment of Freedom Itself, the manifestation of Freedom within the boundaries of an individual form. Freedom moves freely within the boundaries of his form. The Guru simply, spontaneously, in his play, moves in a way that dissipates the dense, congealed energy of the mind. He is said to break the boundaries of the student, to break the boundaries of the mind. Undeniably, his "outrageous" unconventional behavior demonstrates and displays to the student his own mental boundaries.

In this way he serves the student in the highest way, though this experience may prove to be exceedingly uncomfortable for the student. The student's experience could be that all of his values get shattered, all of his attachments and beliefs smashed in the current of true Freedom, which is the Guru's true nature. For the Guru is the embodiment of Freedom itself. Though Freedom has no problem with boundaries, it spontaneously challenges the boundaries at every moment, in every way. The true miracle is that a limited, confined body/mind can contain the unbounded Freedom of the Guru, of Awareness, that animates it. In fact, it cannot.

Surrender

By loosening the grip of the mind, softening and dissipating the congealed consciousness of mind, and by activating the discriminative faculty and then letting it all go through Self inquiry, the Guru can assist the student to experience fully the Truth of who s/he is, the silent still awareness at the core of his Being, beyond all mental activity. This awareness may then be recognized to not be separate from mental activity. It precipitates into thought itself. Awareness is then realized as the backdrop, the foreground, and the substance of all thoughts. It may also be realized to be the substance of all emotions, and all sense perceptions.

As the realization dawns that awareness, consciousness, is all there is, the opportunity arises for the moment-to-moment surrender or dissipation of thought, emotion, perception to its source, the awareness from which it precipitates. As each thought, emotion, perception is experienced and released back to its source, a continual "deepening" of awakening occurs, integrating fully (merging) the boundless with the boundaries, the Self with perceived Other, the Silence of Who One Is with the Activity of experience, where it has never not been. So this perceived merging is realized to be an illusory experience, just as the experience of Awakening itself is. For, in Truth, there has never been any separation of individual from its universal source, no separation of the wave from the ocean. It is only for the wave to realize its essential nature as the ocean while remaining a wave. This deepening continuously and endlessly occurs as long as the physical body persists.

(adapted from Franklin Merrell-Wolff's Experience and Philosophy)

Conclusion

The great Self-Realized sage Ramana Maharishi has said there are two ways to Self Realization.

Either one has to inquire deeply with steadfastness about the arising of the *aham vritti* (the "I" thought – the feeling awareness of I AM), or one must surrender entirely to the Guru that is one's own Self, the very Heart of one's existence.

In either approach, the pure ego, the sense of identity, the "I"-ness, merges in the Heart, and the Self reveals ItSelf to ItSelf.

Ramana often made the point that although spiritual effort is critical, one cannot go beyond a certain point with effort alone, and that Grace is needed.

When asked, how one could obtain Grace, Ramana would say that Grace is ever-existent and always there. One only needs to be aware of It.

That is why Ramana often brought attention to the nature of awareness and its source, the Heart. The fact that Self is Always Realized, and that Grace is eternally present, can be meditated upon.

So one makes a sincere effort, a human effort, and does what is possible. Then Grace takes over, some Power, the Holy Spirit, Power of the Self – that takes the surrendered mind and merges it in the Heart.

The Heart is the magnet. The words of the Guru are Grace because they make the student alert and aware of the eternal divine nature.

When the consciousness of the student is ripe, and all the effort that is possible has been made, through Grace, mind and Shakti are drawn to the Heart, and the Heart swallows up everything. The Supreme Silence beyond time and space shines forth as one's own Self.

Ramana used to say that there is no seeing the Self. There is only Being It.